DATE DUF

DEPRECIATION POLICIES

Depreciation

Policies

and

Resultant

Problems

William T. Hogan, S.J.

STUDIES IN INDUSTRIAL ECONOMICS
NUMBER 8

FORDHAM UNIVERSITY PRESS · NEW YORK

Prefatory Note

Depreciation is of prime importance to American enterprise as a major source of corporate funds. *Depreciation Policies and Resultant Problems* discusses the evolution of depreciation policy and practices and their effect on the economy with respect to capital replacement. Capital replacement, in turn, accounts for modernization of plant and facilities and thus has a pronounced effect on productivity, profits and to some extent, prices.

Developments in the post-World War II period created a problem in regard to capital replacement. Prior to the war, depreciation reserves were quite adequate for the replacement of industrial plant and equipment, but after 1945 a severe erosion of the dollar's purchasing power and an accelerated role of technological advance made it impossible for business to retain sufficient funds through depreciation accruals to finance much-needed renewals. Among the results were inefficiencies in productive techniques, higher costs, lower profits, and often higher prices to the consumer. American products found it increasingly difficult to compete in the world market because depreciation laws in foreign countries were much more liberal than in the United States. In 1962 measures were taken to alleviate this situation when the Treasury moved to shorten the lives on depreciable assets and the Congress passed the 7 percent investment tax credit.

This work presents an analysis of the events leading up to the depreciation problem and its relationship to tax policies from the inception of the income tax laws until the present. It examines the growth of depreciation reserves as a source of corporate funds and the important role played by depreciation in business investment decisions. It contains a thorough survey of the depreciation programs in other countries and reviews the various methods proposed to reform the tax laws governing depreciation in this country. Finally, it discusses comprehensively the measures toward reform that were taken by the Treasury and the Congress in 1962.

* * *

Sincere acknowledgment is made for the generous assistance given for the research on this book by the McKinsey Foundation for

v

Management Research, Inc. The author also wishes to express gratitude to Frank T. Koelble for developing information and in preparing the manuscript. Thanks are also due to Edward Corrigan for his assistance in the work.

Table of Contents

List of Tables

I *Development of Depreciation Policies in the United States*

THE NEED TO KEEP PLANT AND EQUIPMENT as modern as possible is a most pressing one in a competitive economy. This has always been necessary, but today it is much more urgent since the pace of competition, both domestic and foreign, has been stepped up appreciably since the close of the Korean War in 1953.

Foreign manufacturers with plants rebuilt after the destruction and ravages of World War II have at the present time efficient production facilities in the basic industries as well as in the fabricating industries. Further, domestic competition in the United States has become much keener as a result of large expenditures for research and development since the close of World War II. The manifold increase in this outlay is evident from the fact that expenditures in 1946 for R & D were slightly less than one billion dollars while in 1964 they totaled 13.4 billion dollars. This outlay has resulted in new products and processes, as well as improved plant and equipment. The rapid advances in development of plant and equipment have accelerated the rate of obsolescence so that an increasing pressure has been placed on business to modernize its facilities in order to remain competitive. This situation was summed up succinctly by President Kennedy in his Tax Message to Congress in April 1961 as follows:

Today, as we face serious pressure on our balance of payments position, we must give special attention to the modernization of our plant and equipment. Forced to reconstruct after wartime devastation, our friends abroad now possess a modern industrial system helping to make them formidable competitors in world markets. If our own goods are to compete with foreign goods in price and quality, both at home and abroad, we shall need the most efficient plant and equipment.

The problem has been accentuated by the fact that an inflationary trend which has been operative with varying degrees of intensity during the post-World War II period has made it more difficult to replace capital assets with allowable depreciation deductions. Plant and equipment installed before of during World War II must now be replaced at a cost which is two to three times greater than the original. Unfortunately only the original amount which has been written off is available for replacement. Thus, considerable funds must be raised from other sources to make up the deficit. Further, the tax laws up until recently have required that assets be written off over a longer period of time than is consonant with economic obsolescence so that a piece of equipment which may be physically fit to operate is often economically obsolete owing to advances in technology.

These developments have created a problem in regard to capital replacement that did not exist prior to World War II when depreciation reserves were quite adequate for the replacement of capital assets. The problem has been alleviated to a considerable extent by the passage of the Revenue Act of 1962 which provided a tax incentive for investment in new facilities. In addition, the Treasury issued a new ruling shortening the length of time during which an asset could be written off. This ruling, known as *Revenue Procedure 62–21*, which replaced Bulletin F was somewhat hampered by a rather complicated application of a reserve-ratio test but fortunately, this was revised by Treasury decision in early 1965.

HISTORICAL BACKGROUND

While it has always been a practice to depreciate physical assets, a realization of the need to do this from a financial point of view did not arise until the beginning of the industrial revolution since an industrial society is far more cognizant of the depreciation of machinery than an agricultural society. Further, even in an industrial society, the need to set aside specific amounts from the replacement of plant and equipment was not felt until the Government, through its tax policies, levied an income tax on business. Once this tax was in operation, it was necessary to make a careful deduction of all expenses before income or profit was determined and depreciation, or wear and tear on equipment, was one of these expenses.

The American experience with depreciation is relatively new. The first income tax law of 1861 and the subsequent tax laws of the Civil War period and the immediate post-Civil War era completely ignored depreciation in the determination of taxable income. In 1884, the Bell Company sent a circular to its various licensees recommending a uniform system of accounts for telephone companies. The circular recommended the establishment of depreciation reserves, and suggested that depreciation be treated as an operating expense with a composite rate of 10 percent to be applied against equipment.[1] Section 20 of the Interstate Commerce Act of 1894, which was to be declared unconstitutional in 1895, expressly disallowed depreciation.

The first two decades of the twentieth century were characterized by a vacillation in the treatment of the terms depreciation and obsolescence. In the Tariff Act of 1909, Section 38 deals with a corporate excise tax. This act permitted "a reasonable allowance for depreciation of property, if any."[2] Article 4 of Treasury Regulation 30 construed this provision to mean that it provided for the loss in value "that arises from exhaustion, wear and tear, or obsolescence out of the uses to which the property is put."[3]

On January 4, 1909, the Supreme Court first gave clear recognition of the nature of depreciation in its decision in the case of *City of Knoxville v. Knoxville Water Company* 212 US 1 (1909). In its opinion, the Court stated:

Before coming to the question of profit at all the company is entitled to earn a sufficient sum annually to provide not only for current repairs but for making good the depreciation and replacing the parts of the property when they come to the end of their life. The company is not bound to see its property gradually waste, without making provision out of earnings for its replacement. It is entitled to see that from earnings the value of property invested is kept unimpaired, so that at the end of any given term of years the original investment remains as it was at the beginning. It is not only the right of the company to make such a provision, but it is its duty to its bond and stockholders, and, in the case of a public service corporation at least, its plain duty to the public.[4]

The Court's decision recognized depreciation as a legitimate charge in the determination of public utility rates.

With the ratification of the Sixteenth Amendment in 1913, the legal barriers to income taxation were lifted. Immediately after the ratification, the Tariff Act of 1913 was passed on October 3, 1913. This act is frequently referred to as the first modern income tax law. Its section dealing with corporate taxation and the allowable deductions contains a certain ambivalence with respect to depreciation. Subsection B, Section II lists permissible expenses and deductions. The sixth deduction provides for "a reasonable allowance for the exhaustion, wear and tear of property arising out of its use or employment in the business."[5] Subsection G (b) of Section II specifically made allowances for depreciation when listing allowable deductions "including a reasonable allowance for depreciation by use, wear and tear of property."[6] Article 129 of Treasury Regulation 33 permitted a deduction for depreciation in the value of the property "that arises from exhaustion, wear and tear, or obsolescence out of the uses to which the property is put."[7]

Section 5 (a) (7) of the Revenue Act of 1916 omitted the term depreciation and provided for "a reasonable allowance for the exhaustion, wear and tear of property arising out of its use and employment in the business or trade,"[8] Under this act "no deduction on account of obsolescence was allowed except for the 'withdrawal from use of the obsolete equipment.' "[9]

The Revenue Act of 1918 is very similar to the 1916 act in its depreciation provisions but it does provide for obsolescence. Section 214 (a) (8) permits: "A reasonable allowance for the exhaustion, wear and tear of property used in the trade or business, including a reasonable allowance for obsolescence."[10] The evolution of this sentence was interesting. The House draft provided only for an allowance for exhaustion, wear and tear but did not specifically refer to depreciation or obsolescence. When the act reached the Senate, it was amended by substituting depreciation for the clause "exhaustion, wear and tear." In the conference of the House and the Senate, depreciation was deleted and the provision as quoted above was agreed upon.[11]

On August 31, 1920, the Bureau of Internal Revenue in connection with the Revenue Act of 1918 issued the first edition of Bulletin F which dealt with *Depreciation and Obsolescence*. In the introduction to the Bulletin, its purpose and contents are summarized:

The contents of this bulletin indicate the trend and tendency of official opinion in the Bureau of Internal Revenue in administering the portions of the Revenue Act of 1918 which provide for the deduction from gross income of reasonable allowances for exhaustion, wear and tear, and obsolescence of property used in trade or business.

The introduction states further that

the Bureau does not prescribe rates to be used in computing depreciation and obsolescence, as it would be impracticable to determine rates which would be equally applicable to all property of a general class or character. For this reason no table of rates is published. The rate applicable and the adjustment of any case must depend upon the actual conditions existing in that particular case.

The Bulletin very clearly defines both depreciation and obsolescence:

Depreciation means the gradual reduction in the value of property due to physical deterioration, exhaustion, wear and tear, through use in trade or business.

Obsolescence means the gradual reduction in the value of property due to the normal progress of the art in which the property is used, or to the property becoming inadequate to the growing needs of the trade or business. Obsolescence, a gradual lessening of value must be distinguished from "loss of useful value" (art. 143, Reg. 45), which contemplates an abrupt termination of usefulness.[12]

Unlike the succeeding edition of Bulletin F, the original edition gave no guide lines at all as to the length of time over which an asset may be depreciated. In fact, it points out very clearly that this is an extremely difficult judgment to make. Under the section on *Rate of Depreciation— Probable Useful Life of Property*, the following observations are made:

Consideration of the elements entering into depreciation and of the many problems arising therefrom, involves questions of great difficulty, the solution of which does not yield to exact determination in such a manner that precise rules of treatment can be established or theoretical formulae deduced which can be applied to all cases, or even to many. It is considered impracticable to prescribe fixed definite rates of depreciation which would be allowable for all property of a given class or character. The rate at which property depreciates necessarily depends upon its character, locality, purpose for which used, and the conditions under which it is used. Manufacturing plants in the same locality, doing identically the same kind of business, depreciate at widely different rates, to a large extent dependent upon the management and the fidelity with which repairs are made and the property maintained; but so many other elements enter into the question that even the relative importance of the different factors can be determined only with difficulty and as approximations. The taxpayer should in all cases determine as accurately as possible according to his judgment and experience the rate at which his property depreciates. The rate used will, however, be subject to the approval of the Commissioner.[13]

The Internal Revenue Bureau was particularly realistic in recognizing extraordinary condition of manufacture and their effect on plant and equipment. In regard to this, the Bulletin states:

It is recognized also that property, for example, manufacturing machinery, may be subject to extraordinary depreciation due to being operated overtime, at an overload, or being used for some purpose for which it is not adapted. Under such conditions, a taxpayer may deduct in addition to the amount measuring the depreciation under normal conditions, a further sum to provide for the extraordinary depreciation. It does not necessarily follow that if a machine operated normally for 8 hours a day, is operated for 16 hours a day, it will depreciate twice as rapidly as when operated under normal conditions. The estimate of the extraordinary depreciation should be made by the taxpayer according to his judgment and experience and will be subject to the approval of the Commissioner.[14]

In regard to the methods of computing depreciation, the Bureau stated that the method of fixed percentage, or as it is known today, the straight-line method, was acceptable, as was the method for apportioning the life of the equipment over a number of units of production. Other methods, such as declining-balance, re-valuation method, sinking fund method, were not approved in their entirety by the Commissioner for income tax purposes.

Treasury policy remained liberal throughout the 1920s. Rates were in force which in some instances permitted recovery to proceed more rapidly than if governed by durable life. Taxpayers had considerable latitude in write-off selection on the ground that tax advantages gained by high rates of depreciation in the early years of an asset's life would be cancelled out by exhaustion of the allowance. To find a rate unreasonable, the Bureau of Internal Revenue had to present clear and convincing evidence of the unreasonableness. The tax advantage in such rates, however, was minimal as tax rates in general were low.

On December 3, 1933, a subcommittee of the House Ways and Means Committee issued Report No. 704 of the House of Representatives. The report, after careful consideration of the question of depreciation allowances, stated that "such deductions are of alarming size and show continuous increases as are shown by the following figures for corporations:

DEPRECIATION TAKEN ON CORPORATE RETURNS

1924	$2,683,415,617	1928	$3,598,912,546
1925	2,857,710,739	1929	3,870,924,234
1926	3,270,429,583	1930	3,986,208,883
1927	3,346,379,298	1931	4,002,508,000

The depreciation deduction in 1931 is larger than the total taxable net income of all corporations."[15] The subcommittee recommended an arbitrary reduction of 25 percent in the depreciation allowances for a three-year period.

On January 26, 1934, Henry Morgenthau, Jr., Secretary of the Treasury, wrote to Robert L. Doughton, Chairman of the Ways and Means Committee, on this subject. Mr. Morgenthau recommended that the depreciation deductions allowed by the Treasury be handled by administrative decision rather than be incorporated into law. He also suggested that the burden of proof as to whether or not a deduction was unreasonable be shifted from the Treasury Department to the tax payer. The letter, which follows, sums up the thinking of the Treasury Department on this matter.

The Secretary of the Treasury
Washington, January 26, 1934

Hon. Robert L. Doughton
Chairman Committee on Ways and Means
House of Representatives
Washington, D.C.

My Dear Mr. Chairman: In connection with the consideration now being given by the Ways and Means Committee to the inclusion in the pending revenue bill of some provision limiting or restricting the amount of deductions that may be allowed for depreciation, I believe it important that your Committee should be informed regarding the action now proposed by the Bureau of Internal Revenue with respect to that subject.

Section 23 (k) of the Revenue Act of 1932 grants as a deduction "a reasonable allowance for the exhaustion, wear and tear of property used in the trade or business, including a reasonable allowance for obsolescence." In interpreting this section, article 205 of Treasury Regulations 77 provides that "while the burden of proof must rest upon the taxpayer to sustain the deduction taken by him, such deductions will not be disallowed unless shown by clear and convincing evidence to be unreasonable." Acting under these provisions and the corresponding provisions of prior acts and regulations, the Bureau has attempted to check the amount of depreciation deductions taken in income-tax returns by an investigation through its field officers of the records of taxpayers and by the preparation of detailed and often burdensome depreciation schedules, which are ordinarily necessary before judging the reasonableness of the deduction. In proceeding in this manner the Bureau has been handicapped in at least two important respects. First, the volume of this work has been such as to preclude the preparation of proper schedules in many cases. Second, the Bureau has been placed in the position of having to show by clear and convincing evidence that the taxpayer's claim was unreasonable, a particularly difficult matter since the determination of the useful life of the assets and the consequent rates of depreciation is largely within the taxpayer's experience.

The Bureau has for several months had under consideration more effective means of administering the depreciation provisions. This study has shown that through past depreciation deductions many taxpayers have (as shown by facts now known to exist) built up reserves for depreciation which are out of proportion to the prior exhaustion, wear and tear of the depreciable assets. If past methods are continued, the amount representing the basis of the assets will be completely recovered through depreciation deductions before the actual useful life of the assets has been terminated.

In order to overcome this condition the Bureau proposes to reduce substantially the deductions for depreciation with respect to many taxpayers in various industries, so that for the remaining life of the assets depreciation will be in effect reduced to the extent that it may have been excessive in prior years.

It is intended that this end shall be accomplished first, by requiring taxpayers to furnish the detailed schedules of depreciation (heretofore prepared by the Bureau), containing all the facts necessary to a proper determination of depreciation; second, by specifically requiring that all deductions for depreciation shall be limited to such amounts as may reasonably be considered necessary

B

to recover during the remaining useful life of any depreciable asset the unre-covered basis of the asset; and, third, by amending the Treasury regulations to place the burden of sustaining the deductions squarely upon the taxpayers, so that it will no longer be necessary for the Bureau to show by clear and convincing evidence that the taxpayers' deductions are unreasonable. These changes will increase the revenue substantially, and, although difficult to estimate, records indicate that the amount of the increase in revenue will equal that which would result from the proposal of the Ways and Means Committee.

Although the studies of depreciation made in the Bureau bear out the con-clusion of the Ways and Means Committee that as a whole the deductions taken for depreciation in the past has been excessive when considered in the light of the facts now known to exist, it is the opinion of the present Bureau officials that the situation can be more equitably remedied through proper administrative measures than through legislation which would arbitrarily reduce each and every taxpayer's depreciation allowance by a certain percentage, whether or not the allowance may be excessive for past years. I concur in this opinion and I therefore urge that the matter be rested on proper administration rather than on legislative action.

Very truly yours,
H. Morgenthau, Jr.
Secretary of the Treasury

Treasury Decision 4422, issued on February 28, 1934, incorporated the Treasury's changes. This revision of Treasury policy reads in part as follows:

Art. 205 Method of computing depreciation allowance— . . . The deduction for depreciation in respect of any depreciable property for any taxable year shall be limited to such ratable amount as may reasonably be considered necessary to recover during the remaining useful life of the property the unrecovered cost or other basis. The burden of proof will rest upon the taxpayer to sustain the deduction claimed. Therefore, taxpayers must furnish full and complete infor-mation with respect to the cost or other basis which has been recovered through depreciation allowances for prior taxable years, and such other information as the Commissioner may require in substantiation of the deduction claimed.[16]

There was no insistence upon the straight-line method since the capital sum to be recovered could be written off over the asset's useful life "either in equal annual installments or in accordance with any other recognized trade practice, such as an apportionment of the capital sum over the units of production."[17]

On April 4, 1934, Mimeograph 4170 was issued by the Treasury Depart-ment. It gave in considerable detail information concerning the deprecia-tion schedule to be followed by taxpayers in computing the information necessary to substantiate his depreciation deductions.

Although prior experience with the straight-line method revealed underdepreciation during the early years of asset lives, taxpayers were not aggressive in proposing alternative methods and the straight-line write-offs were maintained in almost universal use. Not until the post-World War II period, when rising prices aggravated the incidence of under-depreciation, was the straight-line method subjected to serious attack and solutions such as the declining-balance method of double the rate and the sum of the years' digits method employed.[18]

In the years immediately following 1934, primary concern centered not on the various write-off methods, but on the question of establishing estimated useful lives for various types of assets. If not established by the taxpayer, it become customary for the Bureau to impose lower rates by reference to Bulletin F which now became a catalogue or list of probable useful lives for several hundred assets, which claimed to reflect average experience.[19] Actually, in many cases, Bulletin F tended to overestimate useful life.

A comparison of useful lives of representative refining installations as listed in Bulletin F and the actual experience of the refining operations clearly points out the dichotomy between Bulletin F and reality. Bulletin F's suggested lives for brick warehouse, cracking stills and small compressors were 60, 15 and 10 years respectively, the actual experience of the small refineries was 20, 10 and 5 years respectively.[20]

In addition, provision was not made for extraordinary obsolescence which resulted from unforeseen influences such as technological developments and economic changes which force retirement of capital assets before the termination of useful life. With respect to extraordinary obsolescence, Bulletin F read as follows:

Extraordinary or special obsolescence rarely can be predicted prior to its occurrence. However, this does not necessarily imply that the asset already must have been completely discarded or become useless, but merely that a point has been reached where it can be definitely predicted that its use for the present purpose will be discontinued at a certain future date. Deductions for obsolescence of this type may be taken over the period beginning with the time such obsolescence is apparent and ending with the time the property will become obsolete. In every case the burden of proof is entirely upon the taxpayer to establish a claim for obsolescence by fact and evidence that are definite and indisputable. No amount may be charged off in any year merely because, in the opinion of the taxpayer, property may become obsolete a number of years later. . . . In no case may the deduction for obsolescence be extended to include shrinkage in value due to other causes as for instance, a general drop in the price of commodities.

After twenty years of haggling over depreciation rates, a change in policy was announced on May 12, 1953, when it was stated as follows:

The internal-revenue laws allow as a deduction in computing net income a reasonable allowance for depreciation of property used in trade or business or of property held for the production of income. The purpose of the deduction is to permit taxpayers to recover through annual deductions the cost (or other basis permitted by law) of the property over the useful life of the property. The determination of the amount of the deduction is largely a matter about which there may be reasonable differences of informed judgment, but the impact on the revenues resulting from these differences may be negligible one way or the other over the years involved.

Accordingly, effective May 12, 1953, and as respects all other years for which agreement as to the tax liability has not been reached at any level within the Internal Revenue Service as of that date, it shall be the policy of the Service generally not to disturb depreciation deductions, and revenue employees shall propose adjustments in the depreciation deduction only where there is clear and convincing basis for a change. This policy shall be applied to give effect to its principal purpose of reducing controversies with respect to depreciation.[21]

In 1954, Congress revised the governmental policy toward depreciation when it passed the Internal Revenue Code of 1954. The major revision was the explicit allowance of two additional methods of depreciation, the declining-balance method and the sum of the years' digits method. These two methods will be discussed in detail later in this chapter. Section 167 (c) of the code, however, limited the use of these methods to cases:

... of property (other than intangible property) described in subsection (a) with a useful life of 3 years or more:

(1) the construction, reconstruction, or erection of which is completed after December 31, 1953, and then only to that portion of the basis which is properly attributable to such construction, reconstruction, or erection after December 31, 1953, or

(2) acquired after December 31, 1953, if the original use of such property commences with the taxpayer and commences after such date.

A special announcement dated February 21, 1955 summarized the policy in this area:

1. Effective with the promulgation of the regulations under section 167 of the Internal Revenue Code of 1954, it is the policy of the Internal Revenue Service to determine all questions concerning depreciation in accordance with the Internal Revenue Code and Regulations thereunder without reference to the text of Bulletin "F."

The policy set forth in Revenue Rulings 90 and 91 (CB 1953-1, pp. 43 and 44) will remain in effect and accordingly it will be the policy of the Service generally not to disturb depreciation deductions, and Revenue employees will propose adjustments in the depreciation deductions only where there is a clear and convincing basis for a change, and

Taxpayers are cautioned that the periods of useful life shown in Bulletin "F" are not mandatory, and were published originally solely as a guide to what might be considered reasonably normal periods of useful life.[22]

In July 1962 a significant step was taken by the Treasury Department when it replaced Bulletin F with a completely new schedule determining the length of useful lives. Its central objective was to shorten useful lives on depreciable assets. The provisions of the 1962 tax revision, as well as its 1965 modifications, are discussed in a subsequent section of this book.

METHODS FOR DETERMINING DEPRECIATION

Up to 1954 the method of depreciation used by the vast majority of corporate enterprises was the straight-line method. It has also been referred to in the 1920 edition of Bulletin F as the percentage method. It is true, as previously stated, that the Bureau of Internal Revenue recognized another method, namely, spreading the life of capital equipment over a certain number of units of production. However, this was by no means widely used. After 1954 other methods were permissible, such as the declining-balance and the sum of the years' digits.

Section 167 (b) of the Internal Revenue Code of 1954 enumerates the methods by which depreciation can be calculated for tax purposes. It permits the use of

1. The straight-line method.

2. The declining-balance method, using a rate not exceeding twice the rate which would have been used had the annual allowances been computed under the method described in paragraph 1.

3. The sum of the years' digits method.

4. Any other consistent method productive of an annual allowance which, when added to all allowances for the period commencing with the taxpayer's use of the property and including the taxable year, does not, during the first two-thirds of the useful life of the property, exceed the total of such allowances which would have been used had such allowances been computed under the method described in paragraph 2.

The first three methods are in general use today, and offer advantages to particular types of businesses. There are a number of other methods which are used in a very limited number of instances, which need not be described here.

The straight-line method is still the most simple and widely used of all. It bases depreciation on the original cost of the asset less its terminal or scrap value and distributes the amount to be written off equally over the number of years estimated for the life of the asset. It can be reduced to the following formula:

$$D = \frac{C - T}{N}$$

D is the total amount of depreciation
C represents the original cost
T is the terminal or scrap value of the
asset
N is the number of years over which the
asset is written off or its useful life span.

The method is simple and easily adaptable to any asset, and in fact, has been adopted by many regulatory boards. However, it contains an inherent weakness. It is generally recognized that an asset loses almost two-thirds of its value during the first half of its useful life. This is due primarily to the danger of obsolescence. Therefore, according to the straight-line method in the first half of the asset's life only half of its original value has been reclaimed while its value has actually depreciated two-thirds, so that this method does not represent a realistic means of calculating depreciation.

The second method, namely, the declining-balance method, is not used as frequently as the straight-line method. It is, however, quite popular in a number of industries and is particularly useful for assets with relatively short lives. The method allows a greater amount of depreciation to be taken in the first few years of the asset's life, and thus affords protection against obsolescence due to rapid technological change. In the declining-balance method, the Bureau of Internal Revenue allows the taxpayer to take up to 200 percent of the amount he would have taken if he used the straight-line method.

The following example illustrates the declining-balance method:

On an asset worth $10,000 which is to be depreciated over ten years, the first year's depreciation charge would be double that allowed on the straight-line basis. Thus it would amount to 20 percent. This $2,000 is subtracted from the value of the asset so that for the second year the 20 percent depreciation rate is taken on $8,000 rather than $10,000 and amounts to $1,600. For the third year, the accumulated depreciation of the first two, namely, $3,600, is subtracted from the asset's value so that the 20 percent depreciation rate is taken on a $6,400 base. The following table indicates the depreciation charges for ten years. It will be noted that at the end of that period the full amount of the asset's value is not recovered.

The declining-balance method allows recovery of investment cost to proceed more rapidly in the case of short-lived as opposed to long-lived assets. Where the estimated life of an asset is ten years, for example, slightly more than two-thirds of its cost is recovered during the first half of its estimated life. However, where an asset's life is forty years, only 64.15 percent of its cost is recovered at the end of twenty years.

It will be noted from the example that the amount of depreciation charged off in the last six years declines very rapidly and is considerably less than would be charged off under the straight-line method. In fact, in the last year the annual charge is $268.43 under the declining balance method whereas with the straight-line method it would have been $1,000. Further, in the example cited, the aggregate depreciation is some 11 percent short of the original value of the asset, and unless the asset can be sold or salvaged for $1,000, between 10 and 11 percent of it is not

TABLE 1

AN ILLUSTRATION OF THE DECLINING-BALANCE METHOD OF DEPRECIATION

Year	Annual Charge	Rate	Accumulated Depreciation	Asset Value $10,000
1	$2,000.00	20%	$2,000.00	$8,000.00
2	1,600.00	20	3,600.00	6,400.00
3	1,280.00	20	4,880.00	5,120.00
4	1,024.00	20	5,904,00	4,096.00
5	819.20	20	6,723.20	3,276.80
6	665.38	20	7,388.56	2,621.44
7	534.29	20	7,912.85	2,097.15
8	419.43	20	8,332.28	1,677.72
9	335.54	20	8,667.82	1,342.18
10	268.43	20	8,936.25	1,073.74

recoverable under this method. This would seem to be a definite disadvantage. However, those who use the method feel that the rate of recovery in the first few years more than compensates for this residue which is not charged off.

A third method that can be used under the present tax regulation is the sum of the years' digits. This involves the application of a varying percentage to a fixed base or value. For example: in the case of an asset with an estimated life of five years, the numbers one through five are added and reach the sum of 15. This is the denominator of the fraction to be applied against the value of the asset. On a basis of a five-year life during the first year, $\frac{5}{15}$ths may be written off, in the second year, $\frac{4}{15}$ths, the third year $\frac{3}{15}$ths, the fourth year, $\frac{2}{15}$ths and the last year, $\frac{1}{15}$th. This permits a relatively high recovery during the first few years and again protects the taxpayer against obsolescence due to technological improvements. For example: if an asset had a value of $10,000 and a five-year life, during the first year, $\frac{5}{15}$ths or one-third could be written off. The following table indicates the total write-offs that would take place during five years:

TABLE 2

AN ILLUSTRATION OF THE SUM OF THE YEARS' DIGITS METHOD OF DEPRECIATION

Year	Fraction or Percentage Written Off Yearly	Annual Charge
1	5/15 (33⅓%)	$3,333.33
2	4/15 (26⅔%)	2,666.67
3	3/15 (20%)	2,000.00
4	2/15 (13⅓%)	1,333.33
5	1/15 (6⅔%)	666.67

The amount of accrued depreciation in the firm is determined by the size of the capital expended on plant and equipment and the type of depreciation write-off which is chosen. Within the limits imposed by the Treasury regulations a firm's write-off can vary depending on the policy and practices that its management has in respect to the useful lives of its equipment and the accounting method employed.

Businesses have varied depreciation write-offs depending upon profit considerations and operating rates. A firm with a relatively low profit margin may strive to charge a minimum amount of depreciation in order to lower costs and increase profits. In fact, at times, some firms have made a change in their accounting practices when either profits have been low or losses were incurred so as to minimize costs. Further, in some industries the amount of depreciation written off varies with the operating rate of the industry. In one industry when the operating rate is between 85 and 100 percent, the full depreciation is taken. As the rate drops from 85 to 50 percent, a sliding scale is employed to reduce the amount of depreciation charged. However, at no time does the depreciation write-off fall below 50 percent of that allowed no matter how low the operating rate is. Thus if the operating rate fluctuates between 50 and 85 percent, amounts of depreciation varying between 50 and 100 percent of the allowable are charged off.

Depreciation rates in the firm may also vary depending upon the accounting method adopted and the useful lives assigned to the assets which are depreciated. As has been noted, the tax law allows the firm to choose from three principal methods in depreciating its property. These are the straight-line, declining-balance, and sum of the years' digits approaches. Any other method consistent with the specifications of Section 167 (b) of the Internal Revenue Code of 1954 may also be used.[23] Particularly during the earlier years of an asset's life, the depreciation rate will vary somewhat depending upon the approach taken.

The assignment of useful lives to capital equipment and depreciable assets in general is a basic problem in depreciation accounting. It depends for the most part on engineering estimates and can affect significant variations in the firm's depreciation write-off. The problem involved in useful life determination becomes apparent from a review of depreciation policy development in this regard.

NOTES

[1] Earl A. Saliers, *Depreciation: Principles and Applications* (New York, The Ronald Press Company, 1939), p. 18.

[2] *United States Statutes At Large*, XXXVI, Part I (Washington, 1911), p. 113.

[3] V. Loewers Gambrinus Brewery Company v. Anderson Individually And As Collector of Internal Revenue, 282 US 638, 1930, p. 643.

[4] City of Knoxville v. Knoxville Water Company, 212 US 1909, pp. 13–14.

[5] *United States Statutes at Large*, XXXVIII, Part 1 (Washington, 1915), p. 167.

[6] *United States Statutes At Large*, XXXVIII, Part 1 (Washington, 1915), p. 172.

[7] Gambrinus Brewery Company v. Anderson *loc. cit.*, p. 643.

[8] *United States Statutes At Large*, XXXIX, Part 1 (Washington, 1917), p. 759.

[9] Gambrinus Brewery Company v. Anderson, *loc. cit.*, p. 643.

[10] *United States Statutes At Large*, XL, Part 1 (Washington, 1919), p. 1067.

[11] Gambrinus Brewery Company v. Anderson, *loc. cit.*, p. 643.

[12] *Treasury Department: Bureau of Internal Revenue Bulletin "F" Income Tax* (Washington, 1920), p. 5.

[13] *Ibid.*, pp. 26–27.

[14] *Ibid.*, p. 27.

[15] *House Reports 73 Congress 2nd Session Public*, II, 1934.

[16] Treasury Decision 4422.

[17] *Ibid.*

[18] Use of the two new methods was authorized by the Internal Revenue Code of 1954. Although a significant advance, the new Code did not provide a long-range solution to account for obsolescence induced by the accelerated pace of technological development.

[19] Bulletin F was originally issued in 1920 as a summary of the current official policy on depreciation. In January of 1931, a revised edition was issued and it was accompanied by a separate 34 page document, *Preliminary Report on Depreciation*, which gave the probable useful life and corresponding straight-line depreciation rate for over 2,700 different kinds of industrial assets. Grant

and Norton, *Depreciation* (New York, The Ronald Press Company, 1955), pp. 216–218.

[20] W. L. Nelson "Amortization and Depreciation Rates," *Oil and Gas Journal,* February 3, 1949, p. 90.

[21] Statement released with IR *Mimeo 183* and IR *Circular 145.*

[22] Internal Revenue Release—182.

[23] See page 11, above.

II Depreciation and the Problem of Industrial Obsolescence

THE MODERNIZATION OF PLANT AND EQUIPMENT is an extremely important corporate function and is essential to profitable operations particularly where competition is intense. In 1962, when the Treasury moved to shorten the lives on depreciable assets to permit faster write-offs and speed replacement, from one-quarter to one-third of the nation's manufacturing facilities were economically obsolete. In view of the significance of capital modernization and the steady increase in competition from foreign producers after the mid-1950s, the extent of this obsolescence was sufficient to constitute a crisis situation. It had seriously affected the ability of domestic producers to compete in world markets, and many of them increased their investments abroad where more liberal provisions for capital recovery were offered. Consequently, the fact that stringent depreciation laws had been maintained in the United States had contributed in no small part to the deficit in the nation's balance of payments. Further, the use of obsolete machinery had resulted in higher operating costs, thus leading to higher prices, lower profits, lower productivity and a slower rate of economic growth.

The condition of the nation's plant and equipment has been improved significantly since 1962 when the new depreciation guidelines and the investment tax credit were introduced. During 1962 business expenditures for new plant and equipment increased to a record $37.3 billion, surpassing the previous record level of $35.7 billion established in 1957. The advance continued during 1963 and outlays for the year totaled $39.2 billion, 5.1 percent above the level of 1962.

During the period 1962–1963, investment programs emphasized replacement and modernization rather than capacity additions, since excess capacity persisted in a number of industries. The new depreciation guidelines which were designed to assist the replacement of obsolete facilities had been issued in mid-1962 and the investment credit had been approved later the same year. These measures were retroactive to total 1962 operations, but 1963 was the first year in which they were fully operative. All of the major industry groups, excluding mining and non-rail transportation, participated in the 1963 increase in plant and equipment investment. The largest increases were recorded by durable goods manufacturers, the railroads, communications and commercial firms.

In 1964, investment by industry in new plant and equipment increased by 14.5 percent to $44.9 billion. The primary metals industries, the paper, chemical, and motor vehicle industries increased their capital outlays by sizable amounts. The airlines increased their expenditures after two years of cutbacks, as did the electric and gas utilities following a five-year leveling off in spending. The railroads again increased their expenditures by sizable proportions.

This growth in capital investment was partly a result of the revision of the length of life for capital assets and the investment tax credit provided by the 1962 tax law. However, a number of non-tax stimulants were also operative during the period, particularly after the fourth quarter of 1963. By the start of 1964 the growth in demand led to gains in output and pushed the average utilization rate on capacity from 86 to 88 percent. Profit margins improved and boosted cash flows which were also augmented by increased depreciation write-offs, the investment tax credit and reduced tax rates. This increased the availability of investment capital from internal sources, while at the same time, funds for borrowing were readily available at stable rates of interest.

In 1965 business investment in new plant and equipment increased substantially and totaled $52 billion, up 15.8 percent from 1964 and 51.2 percent from 1961. The emphasis was placed on capacity expansion as compared with replacement or modernization, which were the keynotes of previous capital outlays. A rise in the utilization rate of capacity to 91 percent, contrasted with an average of 85 percent over the preceding ten years, encouraged investment directed at expansion. Although investment during the year was substantial in all industrial sectors, the rise was particularly large in manufacturing. Investment in the non-manufacturing sector was highlighted by continued heavy outlays by the railroads and the transportation group in general.

The growth in investment between 1962 and 1965 has affected the age distribution of the nation's productive machinery, but to date an accurate determination has not been made of the extent to which modernization has occurred. However, it is generally agreed that significant progress has taken place and that the overall situation has been much improved since 1962 when the last comprehensive survey on the age of industrial facilities was published by the McGraw-Hill Department of Economics.[1] At that time, it was determined that one-quarter of total manufacturing capacity was more than 18 years old. This fact had an influence on the Treasury in its action which replaced Bulletin F with a new and more equitable schedule for determining the useful lives of depreciable assets.

THE MCGRAW-HILL SURVEY AND INDUSTRIAL OBSOLESCENCE

The McGraw-Hill survey published in 1962 included a comparison of the age distribution of productive capacity in the United States in 1957 with that at the end of 1961. The results indicated a significant improvement in the age distribution of productive capacity over the four-year period, and thus demonstrated that businessmen had recognized the necessity for modernizing plant and equipment. However, it was also revealed that one-fourth of our manufacturing capacity was still 16 or more years old. The study covered not only mining and manufacturing, but also the petroleum industry, transportation and communications, electric utilities, as well as finance, trade and services.

It was found that as of December 1961, 24 percent of manufacturing capacity in the United States was installed before the end of 1945. Although it was disconcerting that one-quarter of our domestic manufacturing capacity was over 16 years old, this represented a marked improvement over what had been found in the 1958 survey. At that time, 48 percent of domestic manufacturing capacity had been installed before December 1945.

The fact that one-quarter of domestic manufacturing capacity was installed before the end of 1945 did not mean that each industry, or firm, had this ratio of old to new capacity. Much of the problem of obsolescence stemmed from the fact that many firms in an industry were not as modern as their competitors. The older and smaller firms tended to lag behind the larger firms in introducing new capacity,[2] which caused inequities and inefficiencies in productive techniques.

The survey indicated that about 16 percent of then current manufacturing capacity was installed between 1945 and December 1950. Between December 1950 and December 1956, 27 percent was put in place and between December 1956 and December 1961, the latest five-year period covered by the survey, 33 percent of then current manufacturing capacity was installed. This marked a record of achievement for the business community in updating the quality and quantity of its manufacturing capacity.

In contrast to the earlier periods much of the expanded capacity between 1958 and 1962 was a product of modernization expenditures. The relatively slow pace of economic growth after the mid-1950s, combined with the rapid expansion of capacity in 1956 and 1957, produced excess capacity in the post-1958 period, and thus industry concentrated on modernizing its productive capacity. Because of the vast strides in technology, the replacement facilities were much more productive than the pre-war, outmoded and inefficient plant and equipment which was retired.

It was not entirely clear whether as much modernization took place in the 1958 to 1962 period as was indicated by the survey. On this point McGraw-Hill stated:

These are the results as reported in this particular survey. However, they should be used cautiously for analytical purposes. Companies that participate in the McGraw-Hill survey are generally the larger companies in their industries, and this fact may affect the results. It is possible that very small and medium-sized companies may not have replaced their obsolete and antiquated facilities to the same degree as did large companies because of lack of financial resources, access to the financial markets or cost factors. But even used as a very rough gauge, it is evident that the concentration on modernization has resulted in the abandonment of a large portion of producing facilities which were no longer economic. [3]

Thus the estimates of the age distribution of our productive facilities possibly tended to show too much capacity as new. Therefore, it was entirely probable that more than one-quarter of our domestic manufacturing capacity was installed prior to 1946.

Such capacity estimates even though not completely accurate, do perform a needed service in the study of depreciation problems. The study of the age distribution of capacity shows when and where problems tend to develop. If it is possible to ascertain the point at which a spurt in capacity took place, it may be possible to estimate when the plant and equipment will be replaced and when the problem of inadequate depreciation reserves will have serious effects on an industry.

The table below presents the findings of McGraw-Hill's 1958 and 1962 surveys on the age distribution of industrial capacity.

The highest degree of modernization shown by any industry during the four-year period between the two surveys was recorded in the automobile, truck and parts industry. As of December 1957, 42 percent of all capacity was installed before 1946. In the course of the next four years much of this inefficient capacity was retired so that by December 1961,

TABLE 3

AGE OF INDUSTRIAL CAPACITY

	1958 Survey Percentage Installed			1962 Survey Percentage Installed			
	Prior to Dec. 1945	Dec. 1945 to Dec. 1950	Dec. 1950 to Dec. 1957	Prior to Dec. 1945	Dec. 1945 to Dec. 1950	Dec. 1950 to Dec. 1956	Dec. 1956 to Dec. 1961
INDUSTRY							
Iron and Steel	47	16	37	27	10	29	34
Nonferrous Metals	47	13	40	21	13	31	35
Machinery	41	21	38	24	17	27	32
Electrical Machinery	34	18	48	18	12	25	45
Autos, Trucks and Parts	42	11	47	8	13	50	29
Transportation Equipment	59	9	32	NA	NA	NA	NA
Aircraft	NA	NA	NA	17	11	28	44
Other Transportation Equipment	NA	NA	NA	43	13	18	26
Fabricated Metals and Instruments	54	17	29	25	13	29	33
Chemicals	30	23	47	21	15	31	33
Paper and Pulp	49	17	34	23	16	30	31
Rubber	46	9	45	23	17	28	32
Stone, Clay and Glass	46	20	34	23	15	30	32
Petroleum and Coal Products	45	26	29	20	12	30	38
Food and Beverages	58	19	23	26	19	26	29
Textiles	59	18	23	32	17	24	27
Miscellaneous Manufacturing	51	21	28	28	19	23	30
ALL MANUFACTURING	48	19	33	24	16	27	33
Mining	NA	NA	NA	24	14	33	29
Railroads	NA	NA	NA	39	19	23	19
Other Transportation and Communications	NA	NA	NA	19	15	22	44
Electric Utilities	NA	NA	NA	23	13	29	35
ALL INDUSTRY*	NA	NA	NA	24	16	27	34

NA = Not Available

* Does not include commercial business or gas utilities
Source: *15th Annual McGraw-Hill Survey*, cf. Note 1.

only 8 percent of the industry's capacity was installed prior to 1946.

The reason for this extremely favourable rate of modernization goes back to the boom automobile year of 1955. While the industry produced 7.9 million cars that year, it discovered that operations at this volume involved a number of inefficiencies.[4] Thus, the industry embarked on a replacement and expansion program in order to be able to handle a heavy volume of production efficiently. Another reason for the modern facilities in the automobile and allied products industries was the strong competition among the large producers. In an effort to produce a higher quality product, the large producers exerted pressure on their suppliers for only the highest quality parts and equipment. To supply the public with a superior product, the producers and parts manufacturers had to modernize and update their productive facilities.

Another basic industry in the economy, iron and steel manufacturing, posted a less impressive record in the same four-year period. At the end of December 1961 with extensive modernization and replacement programs under way, only 27 percent of the industry's capacity was installed prior to 1946. This meant that a considerable portion of the industry's older, high cost facilities were modernized or retired. However, relative to all manufacturing industries, the iron and steel industry's standing declined. By the end of 1961 only 24 percent of all manufacturing capacity was pre-1946. Thus while the 1958 survey showed steel slightly better than all manufacturing (47 percent 1946 vs. 48 percent), the second survey indicated that iron and steel fell behind the modernization rate of all manufacturing (27 percent installed before 1946 vs. 24 percent for all manufacturing).

The industry which showed the largest amount of then current capacity installed in the latest five-year period covered, December 1956 to December 1961, was the electrical equipment manufacturing industry. This industry was characterized by a high concentration of new facilities because the customers for its products had themselves shown an eagerness to expand capacity. As can be observed from Table 3, the communications industry, the aircraft industry and the electric utilities industry also had a high percentage of their capacity installed in the 1957–1961 period.

In the electrical machinery industry the problem of insufficient depreciation reserves did not appear to be too pressing since it was a growth industry. Thus the high level of current investment generated high depreciation reserves. Further, as a growth industry it was not burdened with an excessive amount of uneconomical facilities. This was and is generally true of other rapidly growing industries.

The industry which was most heavily dependent upon pre-1946 facilities was the other transportation equipment industry dominated by the manufacturers of railroad rolling stock. These producers were operating 43 percent of their facilities installed before December 1945. No comparative figures are available showing the age distribution of their capacity at the end of 1947. Compared to the other manufacturing industries in the study, this industry installed the lowest amount of capacity in the 1957–1961 period. This was in part due to the low level of production of railroad cars in the post-1957 period. Table 4 indicates that the Federal Reserve Board index of industrial production of railroad equipment was weak after the base year of 1957. Output before that time was stimulated by the production of cars ordered under certificates of necessity at the end of the Korean War. With such weakness in demand it is understandable that railroad car producers were reluctant to expand capacity.

The age distribution of the productive capacity of the petroleum and coal products industry was more favorable than the average of all manufacturing industries. This was true in both the 1958 and 1962 surveys. As of December 1961, only 20 percent of the capacity of this industry was installed before 1946, and 38 percent was installed in the 1957–1961 period.

The manufacturing industry with the second oldest capacity, after other transportation equipment, was the textile industry. It included a number of small producers in addition to the larger companies and was plagued by poor profits and intensive foreign competition. In order to compete with inexpensive foreign textiles, it was essential that the domestic industry modernize its inefficient capacity. Prior to the Bulletin F revision, the President granted special relief to the textile industry in the form of a revision of useful life estimates on textile machinery.

Other industries which had a larger proportion of their capacity in pre-1946 installations than the average of all manufacturing industries tended to be those composed of smaller firms. These firms were restricted in their attempts to augment insufficient depreciation reserves. This tended to be true among such industries as fabricated metals and instruments, food and beverages, and miscellaneous manufacturing. Often it was only the larger companies which could easily raise the needed funds to modernize their plant and equipment to insure efficient, low-cost capacity.

The problem of older high-cost facilities varied from industry to industry. Thus to speak of averages for all industries is actually meaningless. Similarly in speaking of one industry, the average does not apply to each firm within the industry.

Although business firms carried out programs of modernization, particularly after 1958, by 1962 there was still a disadvantageous mixture of modern and obsolete equipment in many plants. In some instances the

C

very latest machinery operated side by side with out-moded and antiquated facilities. As a consequence, the old machinery acted as a bottleneck to the efficient flow of materials thereby hampering and restricting the output of the newer installations. Thus the new facilities could not produce at maximum efficiency, and at times of less than capacity operations it was difficult to use only the modern equipment to take advantage of its cost of operation. In instances where this could be done, substantial savings were realized and resulted in attractive profits even at low rates of operations.

In some cases, many old plants and facilities could not be adapted to new technology, so that if the firm wished to introduce modern methods the antiquated installations had to be scrapped. This posed a further obstacle to modernization for in such instances the change had to be all

TABLE 4

RAILROAD EQUIPMENT PRODUCTION
1957 = 100

Year	Locomotives	Freight Cars
1957	100.0	100.0
1958	74.5	42.3
1959	88.5	37.6
1960	80.0	56.9
1961	75.4	31.7

Source: Federal Reserve Board.

or nothing. The use of old facilities also cut down on productivity, particularly in those cases just mentioned where new equipment and the old facilities were integrated in the same plant.

Another study dealing with the problem of the obsolescence of productive capacity was completed in 1959 by Johns Hopkins University. This study dealt principally with machine tools used in the production of weapons for the armed forces. The conclusions indicated a high degree of obsolescence in the machine tools held by the Army, as well as those used by contractors who were engaged in defense work. A recommendation was made that from 750 to 2,000 machine tools should be purchased annually for at least five years in order to maintain a minimum level of efficiency.

The study highlighted the fact that technology in the production of machine tools was advancing rapidly. Newer machine tools offered a higher level of precision and had the ability in a metalworking operation to remove metal five to ten times faster than the tools in use before 1940. Each advance in the continuing increase in technological knowledge was making more of the older machinery obsolete. Because of these innovations and the continual research and development in the field, the economic life of a tool was cut from the pre-war standard of 15 to 20 years to an estimated 6 to 10 years. In fact, one comment on the survey stated that it "has gone on record with the belief that new equipment should be replaced in less than 10 years from its installation date. If that is not done, introduction of a new technology will suffer intolerable delays."[5] Many of the then current machine tools were capable of performing satisfactorily for more than ten years. Nevertheless the problem was one of competition and a more modern tool, if it was substantially superior to its earlier counterpart, rendered it obsolete, economically speaking, even though the older tool was operating at or near its original potential. The machine tool industry was characterized by rapid technological advances which in many instances involved a high degree of automation resulting in a substantial reduction in the cost of operation. Thus it was extremely difficult to assign a number of years of economic life to a machine tool in advance. Nevertheless the estimate of 6 to 10 years seemed to be a relatively reasonable one.

In June 1963, McGraw-Hill published *The Ninth American Machinist Inventory of Metalworking Equipment.* Its findings were that two out of every three machine tools in metalworking (64 percent) were at least ten years old. This was an all-time high for the post-war period and compared with a 20 percent rate in 1958. The percentage increased continuously after the close of World War II when 38 percent of machine tools were at least ten years old. The findings of the survey by industry group were as shown on p. 26.

In addition to the McGraw-Hill and Johns Hopkins studies reviewed here, the subject of obsolescence and capital replacement also was treated in a number of careful and thorough studies by the Machinery and Allied Products Institute, under the direction of Dr. George Terborgh.[6]

EXAMPLES OF OBSOLESCENCE IN FOUR INDUSTRIES

The relatively general conclusion of these studies can be highlighted by a consideration of specific instances of obsolescence. Examples have been chosen from four industries, namely, lithography, textiles, railroads and steel. They each had their particular problems, but along with many other industries in the economy they faced the common problem of too much obsolete equipment and not enough funds to modernize to the desired degree.

Lithography

A survey of the lithography industry indicated that a substantial amount of its press equipment in operation at the end of 1961 was economically obsolete. The figure was put as high as 60 percent; in fact by the standards of the industry, machinery that was 10 or more years old was regarded as obsolete and approximately 50 percent of the equipment that had been put in place since World War II was regarded as outmoded.

The operating test of obsolescence was based on the number of net

TABLE 5

PERCENTAGE OF MACHINE TOOLS, AT LEAST 10 YEARS OLD, ON AN
INDUSTRIAL BASIS (1962)

U.S. Industry Group	Percentage of Machine Tools at least 10 years old
Ordnance and Accessories	65
Furniture and Fixtures	58
Primary Metals Industries	69
Fabricated Metal Products	65
Machinery Except Electrical	67
Electrical Machinery and Equipment	54
Transportation Equipment	66
Precision Instruments	56
Miscellaneous Manufacturing	61
All Industry Average	64

impressions produced per press, per chargeable hour. This was not the running speed or maximum speed, it was the actual amount of production that could be turned out when all the factors of preparation including wash up, clean up and make-ready were considered.

A survey of equipment purchased in 1951 vs. that purchased in 1961 indicated the rapid technological progress made in this field as well as the relative costs.

Part of the increase in net impressions per chargeable hour was due to the fact that the new presses reduced make-ready time by approximately 25 percent to 35 percent, i.e., the set-up time for preparing a job to run. In addition to the increase in net production per chargeable hour, there was an estimated 40 to 50 percent increase in quality.

TABLE 6

PRESS EQUIPMENT IN THE LITHOGRAPHY INDUSTRY: COSTS AND TECHNICAL
ADVANCES, 1951 vs. 1961

Item of Equipment	Net 1951 Impressions per Chargeable Hour	Cost	Net 1961 Impressions per Chargeable Hour	Cost
1. Large Equipment—Four Color 72″-76″-77″ Presses	2,400	$210,000	3,200	$340,000
2. Medium Equipment— Two Color 60″ Presses	2,900	90,000	3,800	150,000
3. Small Equipment—Single Color Presses under 30″	3,800	17,500	4,500	26,000

Source: Lithographers & Printers National Association, Inc.

Textiles

The textile industry offered a prime example of a business operating a large amount of obsolete equipment. Table 7 indicates an almost astonishing degree of old age in the industry's production facilities which were being operated in 1960. The serious problem of obsolescence which is apparent was brought on in great part by the lack of funds to replace old

TABLE 7

THE MACHINE REPLACEMENT PATTERN OF THE AMERICAN TEXTILE INDUSTRY

Machines in Place—1960—and Approximate Period of Installation

MACHINES	1960–1950	1950–1940	1940–1920	Older than 1920	Total in Place
Pickers	14.01%	17.34%	32.84%	35.81%	100%
Cards	10.	9.	8.	73.	100
Drawing	15.39	30.25	43.36	11.	100
Combers	23.84	55.15	11.45	9.56	100
Roving	27.03	35.35	27.86	9.76	100
Spinning	19.3	21.66	37.46	21.58	100
Looms	25.	30.	18.	27.	100

Source: American Textile Machinery Association.

equipment. In fact, annual expenditures for new equipment by the industry declined from 510 million dollars in 1947 to 252 million dollars in 1958, a drop of over 50 percent. This decline was particularly startling when one considers that the textile machinery industry was maintaining an active research and development program and had developed equipment which if installed would have led to a reduction in man-hour requirements and operating costs. The industry was anxious to install such machinery and to modernize as much as possible, but it was deterred from doing so because of outmoded depreciation rates which retarded rather than stimulated capital investment.

The condition was recognized by the Administration in Washington and, in May of 1961, President Kennedy announced a program of assistance to the textile industry designed to meet the problems it faced, particularly as a result of technological change. A seven-point program was proposed. In his second point President Kennedy said:

I have asked the Treasury Department to review existing depreciation allowances on textile machinery. Revisions of these allowances, together with adoption of the investment incentive credit proposals contained in my message to the Congress of April 20, 1961, should assist in the modernization of the industry.

As a result of this investigation, the Treasury Department revised the useful lives on textile machinery and equipment by reducing them from 25 years to 15 years and in some cases 12 years. This accelerated depreciation deductions and permitted the industry to modernize to a greater degree.

Some indication of the degree of intensity of obsolescence in the industry prior to the time relief was granted can be had from the fact that a comparison between mills operating equipment in 1950 and those with facilities installed in 1957 indicated on many units a reduction of one-half to three-quarters of payroll cost for an identical amount of production. For instance, in the plant with 1957 equipment, 360 looms attended by 9 employees, accounted for the same amount of production that 500 looms attended by 17 employees turned out in 1950. The difference in pay-roll costs between the two facilities was 47 percent.

The new depreciation guidelines became effective in the textile industry earlier than in other industries and consequently they had a greater impact on 1962 expenditures for textile equipment in comparison with other types of industrial machinery. In 1962 the industry's expenditures for new plant and equipment increased by 18 percent to $610 million. Between 1962 and 1965 this rate of increase was more than sustained and averaged 20.8 percent on an annual basis. During 1965 expenditures rose

32 percent to $990 million which was almost double the total of $500 million spent for new plant and equipment in 1961. As a result of these expenditures the textile industry of today is much more modern than it was in 1961–1962.

Railroads

During the 1950s the railroads, like the textile industry, were gradually beset by a fairly high degree of obsolescence in their plant and equipment. The principal reasons for this were the general declining position of the railroads in relation to passenger and freight traffic and the fact that management in some instances was slow to respond to new situations. These two factors, among others, led to a deterioration in the financial condition of the railroad industry after World War II. In addition, the depreciation tax policy worsened their position so that in many instances

TABLE 8

THE RAILROAD INDUSTRY: NET INCOME AFTER TAXES, 1955–1960

1955	$927,000,000
1956	876,000,000
1957	737,000,000
1958	602,000,000
1959	578,000,000
1960	445,000,000

Source: American Association of Railroads.

they were compelled to continue to use economically outmoded facilities. Further, inflation diminished the real worth of railroads' declining income and made it impossible in many cases to replace assets on which only the original cost had been recouped over a long period of time. The following table, which presents net income after taxes during 1955–1960 indicates the worsening position of the railroads during that period.

This financial situation was particularly unfortunate since it prevented the industry from taking advantage of a number of technological breakthroughs that had been achieved. In fact, techniques in some phases of railroading had advanced so rapidly that even the most recently installed equipment had become economically obsolete long before it was physically worn out.

One of the most outstanding examples of this was the Diesel locomotive. This piece of equipment was relatively new to the railroads. In fact, a large percentage of the locomotives were acquired after 1946. In that year, Class I Railroads had 42,481 locomotives in service, of these 37,551 were steam and only 4,441 were Diesel electric units, while the remainder were electric locomotives. In 1960, the Class I Railroad had 29,180 locomotives in operation of which 28,278 were Diesel electric and only 261 were steam. Thus in a short period of fourteen years, the Diesel locomotive had taken over the task of moving the nation's passenger and freight trains.

Technological change in the Diesel was constant to the point where the General Motors Corporation, the largest producer of Diesel locomotives, made 25 substantial changes in models between 1945 and 1960. Thus the newest units were so much more efficient that a large part of the existing Diesel fleet, which ranged in age from 7 to 11 years, was ready for either major repair or replacement by the improved, more modern and economical units that had been developed. This constituted an example of obsolescence which was truly surprising for the Diesel locomotive was one of the latest developments in the railroad industry and had done much to improve operating costs and performance.

A glaring example of obsolescence which was not evident to the layman was the railroad classification yard for assembling freight trains. A new type yard, known as the Retarder Classification Yard, was developed and employed electronic push-button devices. One railroad installed this equipment in 1953 at a cost of $1.4 million for the electronics and $7 million for the whole yard. Within two years the electronic equipment was rendered obsolete by new developments. This was one of 45 so-called push-button or electronic classification yards and many of these did not have the very latest equipment. However, they were modern compared with 450 other yards whose operations were thoroughly outmoded. Thus only 10 percent of the railroad classification yards in the country could be considered up to date. The remaining 90 percent required considerable funds for modernization.

Another area of railroad obsolescence was in traffic control. The latest development was Central Traffic Control which made for a far more efficient and less costly operation since in some cases it permitted 50 percent more traffic to be handled expeditiously on a single track than did other types of signals. In January 1961, there were only 35,997 miles of track operated under C.T.C. At least another 100,000 miles of track should have been operated by C.T.C., but the funds were not available to make the installation.

In 1962 the railroads initiated programs to regain traffic lost to other carriers by investing heavily in new freight cars and other modern equipment to provide improved service to customers. As an industry, the railroads accounted for the largest relative gain in plant and equipment in 1962 and 1963. In 1962 expenditures by the railroads increased to $850 million, up 26.9 percent from 1961, and in 1963 spending rose by an additional 29.4 percent to $1.1 billion. During 1964 and 1965 spending for new railroad equipment totaled $1.41 and $1.68 billion respectively. The total figure for 1965 was 52.7 percent above that for 1963.

An indication of the extent to which the industry replaced its rolling stock after 1962 can be obtained from statistics on the number of new freight cars and diesel locomotives placed in service. This information is presented in Table 9.

TABLE 9

NEW FREIGHT CARS AND DIESEL LOCOMOTIVES PLACED IN SERVICE
1962–1965

	Freight Cars	Diesel Locomotives
1962	29,287	754
1963	33,770	806
1964	65,801	1,116
1965	68,000	1,450
Total	196,858	4,126

Source: Association of American Railroads.

Steel

The steel industry had spent a number of billions of dollars on replacement and expansion in the post-war period prior to 1962, but in spite of this investment there was still a fair amount of obsolescence. Significant technological advances had occurred in steel operations which rendered many installations obsolete. In addition, the rate of obsolescence was compounded by a number of facilities which had been installed in the late 1920s and 1930s and were still in operation.

Significant examples of obsolescence were to be found in the industry's bar and rod mills. An examination of the performance of this type of mill in regard to productivity and cost revealed that the dividing line between modernity and obsolescence was 1946. With this date as the cutoff point, we find that 59 percent of the mills were installed before that time and thus 41 percent could be considered modern.

In the blast furnace segment of the industry, size of furnace hearth is one criterion of modernity for this operation requires the production of great tonnages to make it efficient and profitable. Most operating men were of the opinion that a furnace with a hearth diameter of less than 25 feet was non-competitive, and 47½ percent of the blast furnace capacity in the steel industry as of January 1960 was in the non-competitive class.

Like the Diesel on the railroads, the steel industry also had its glamor facility, the continuous hot strip mill which was a revolutionary development in the mid-1920s and early 1930s. The developments on this mill were so pronounced that most of them had to be rebuilt or extensively renovated after 1947. Of the 36 wide strip mills in operation in 1960, 15 were built after 1947, another 17 were rebuilt since that date and only 4 were not modernized. Thus a relatively small portion of these mills was obsolete, and yet the percentage would have been much higher had not $20 to $50 million been spent on each of the facilities that were modernized.

In 1962, the year in which the new depreciation guidelines and the investment tax credit were introduced, plant and equipment expenditures in the steel industry moved contrary to the overall trend and declined by 5.3 percent to $911.4 million. With the changes in the law, the industry's depreciation write-offs increased by about 25 percent during the year, but undistributed profits, the other internal source of funds for investment, declined by about 55 percent from $133 million to $59 million, less than 9 percent of what they were in the peak year 1955. By contrast, undistributed profits for all private corporations increased from $6.5 to $8.1 billion. Further, the industry's return on sales which had been on a steady downtrend after 1955, when a 7.8 percent rate was recorded, declined to 4.1 percent from 5.2 percent a year earlier.

Between 1962 and 1965 steel industry expenditures for new plant and equipment increased steadily. In 1963 they totaled $1.04 billion and in 1964 increased by 52.8 percent to $1.59 billion. In 1965 total capital spending reached $1.9 billion, up 19.2 percent from 1964. Much of this spending was for modern facilities for flat-rolled products and for a considerable amount of modern oxygen steelmaking capacity.

Since 1962 some 11 new hot strip mills have been installed or are in the process of installation throughout the industry. In addition to these, a number of cold reduction mills have been put into operation within the last three years. Total capacity of the new hot strip mills will be in the neighborhood of 45 million tons and the product will be of the highest quality because of the excellence of the mills. In fact, it will be the means by which the American steel industry can ward off competition from abroad in the sheet segment of the steel business. In regard to oxygen steelmaking, capacity in the United States increased from 10 million tons in September of 1963 to 17 million tons in 1964 and in 1965 over 22 million tons were actually produced. In addition to these improvements large sums have been spent for taconite beneficiating plants. Thus steel facilities have been modernized to a significant extent since the institution of the investment tax credit.

CAUSES OF OBSOLESCENCE

As previously indicated the basic reason why so high a percentage of industrial capacity became obsolete was that industry did not have sufficient funds to modernize and replace its older high-cost facilities. This deficiency of funds largely resulted from the fact that depreciation charges permitted under the tax laws were inadequate to provide for the replacement of capital equipment. There are two reasons why depreciation reserves were inadequate. In the first place, tax laws and Treasury policy did not make adequate provision for the inflationary trend that had developed in the economy after World War II. Secondly rapid advances in machine technology made the profitable economic life of an asset much less than its physical life, so the asset had to be replaced sooner if the firm was to remain competitive.

The more important of the two causes was that depreciation reserves were insufficient because of the inflationary trend of prices. This brought about increased costs of plant and equipment and a decline in the purchasing power of funds built up in depreciation reserves. Depreciation reserves permitted the companies to recapture, before taxes, the original cost of their facilities. But with inflation the cost of replacing the facilities was substantially above their original cost. Since depreciation reserves recaptured only the original cost, these reserves were insufficient to replace the obsolete plant and equipment at inflated price levels.

The index of construction costs, as tabulated by *Engineering News Record*, serves to illustrate this point. The index increased from 236 (1910–1914 = 100) in 1939 to 824 in 1961, or approximately 250 percent. In other words, the value of the construction dollar which related to equipment installation declined over this period to 30 cents.[7] This rising cost trend presented a serious problem in the replacement of worn-out facilities, for generally speaking, equipment installed in 1939 at a cost of $1 million could not be replaced for less than $2.5 to $3 million. Yet, the depreciation funds which the tax laws permitted to be set aside for this replacement only amounted to the original cost of $1 million. At least an additional $1.5 million had to be obtained elsewhere if the equipment was to be replaced and efficient operations maintained. This problem was felt by all industries employing long-lived equipment written off over a twenty- to thirty-year period. Thus the plant and equipment installed at the start of the 1940s and earlier sustained the full impact of the post-war inflation. The insufficiency of depreciation reserves was most significant for the older, highly capitalized industries and a major cause of obsolescence.

The critical nature of the problem of insufficient depreciation reserves was recognized by a few companies in the years immediately after the war, but many hoped that the inflation would come to an end quickly as it did after World War I. If this would have occurred the difficulty would have been resolved. But the opposite was the case and the inflationary pressures continued to grow. After World War I the wholesale price index of building materials rose from 98 in 1918 (1926 = 100) to 150 in 1920, then broke sharply to 97 in 1921. By contrast, the same index after World War II rose from 118 in 1945 to 224 in 1952 and then continued to increase. An exact comparison was not available since the basis of the index was changed in 1952.

Some specific comparisons of machinery and equipment costs may serve to bring the problem into sharper focus. In 1940 the railroads paid $2,550 for a 55-ton capacity freight car. In 1963, the price of the same capacity car stood at $9,000. A blast furnace, the basic production unit in the steel industry, could be installed for $8 million in 1945. In 1963 the same furnace could not be built for less than $26 million.

In order to replace its worn-out facilities one steel company during a ten-year period had to supplement every dollar invested from depreciation accruals with $1.30 taken from profits. As a result, $220 million had to be drawn from profits to supplement $170 million of depreciation allowances.

The extent of the insufficiency of depreciation reserves was estimated by the Machinery and Allied Products Institute. They attempted to measure the amount of under-depreciation as the excess of current dollar depreciation which they calculated over the historical cost depreciation. This gave the annual value of the deficiency in depreciation reserves because it showed what should be added to the historical depreciation reserves to reflect realistically the cost of replacing plant and equipment. The extent of the insufficiency in depreciation reserves was estimated to be running at a record $5 to $8 billion a year.[8] Deficiencies amounting to this magnitude had been piling up since World War II. Thus the problem of the insufficiency of depreciation reserves due to inflation was one of large proportion.

The inadequacy of depreciation reserves was not caused only by the inflationary trend of the postwar period. The problem which inflation poses to the replacement of worn-out equipment was compounded by another postwar phenomenon, viz., an acceleration in the rate of technological progress. Technological advances embodied in newer machinery tended to make older models of the same type of equipment obsolete before they were fully depreciated. As has been indicated previously, machine tools which once had a useful life of 15 to 20 years were considered obsolete in 6 to 10 years. When the machinery became economically obsolete before it was physically worn out, only a portion of its original cost was set aside in depreciation reserves. Thus the replacement of machinery at the time of its economic obsolescence involved an even greater hardship.

The development of new processes and machinery derived in great measure from the postwar emphasis on research and development and served to increase the rate at which productive equipment became obsolete. Between 1945 and 1959 spending by private industry on research and development increased from $990,000,000 to 9.4 billion dollars.[9] By 1962 the figure had reached $12 billion. These expenditures resulted in new and improved machinery and products. In its 1962 survey, McGraw-Hill discovered that manufacturers expected that by 1965, 14 percent of their sales would come from new or substantially altered products.[10] With this rapid introduction of new and technologically superior equipment, older equipment became economically obsolete in a shorter period of time.

While the problem of inflation can be quantified approximately for study and investigation, the problem raised by technological obsolescence is not as readily measurable. The determination of obsolescence is in great part arbitrary for no one can predict just how long it will be before a new facility is developed to replace an existing one, or just when an existing facility is obsolete. If no further technological advances are made once a machine has been installed, then its economic life will be equal to its physical life. On the other hand, an innovation may render it obsolete in a matter of months. There is no way of predicting the timing of a technological advance, or its corollary, the rendering of present capacity obsolete.

When a technological advance has been discovered and applied, it is difficult even then to say that older installations have been rendered obsolete. Granted that newer techniques, embodied in newer facilities, are more efficient, at what point does the new machinery render the older facilities obsolete? It may be argued that a machine which is 10 percent less efficient than a new facility is, or is not, obsolete.

It would seem that the determination of obsolescence and the economic life of an asset is more than a strict engineering and cost accounting problem. No objective standards exist in determining whether or not a facility is obsolete. However, the following considerations should assist in any judgment on obsolescence: 1. Whether or not firms which are competitors have installed the new equipment. 2. The effect upon the firm's income of a changeover to a newly developed and improved facility. 3. The physical life of the asset which is in operation.

All of these factors apply in various proportions to the problem of obsolescence in any particular instance. However, each instance must be judged on its own merits. If on the average, on the macroeconomic level, productivity gains annually amount to 2 to 3 percent, then it may be said that machinery in general is about 10 to 15 percent more efficient than machinery installed five years before. However, this is a generality which would not apply to any individual machine or group of machinery. But on a macroeconomic scale it may be indicative of the trend in obsolescence. Thus even machinery which is only five years old may be obsolete, depending upon the conditions prevalent in each industry. Certainly installations a decade old or older must be considered economically inferior to new facilities, and may be economically obsolete. Even if one could set standards for determining the obsolescence of installed facilities, it would be impossible to write these into law, stating that economic obsolescence from technological advances was expected to occur in a stipulated number of years. The timing of the introduction of innovations can neither be forecast nor contained.

The problem of financing equipment replacement was temporarily alleviated under the Defense Production Act of 1940 which allowed a five-year write-off of war and defense plants. This was discontinued after World War II, but was revived for the Korean War and remained in operation until 1956 when it was again discontinued. The Internal Revenue Code of 1954 allows for the application of liberalized methods for calculating depreciation, but did not provide a long-range solution for inflation or obsolescence due to technological change. Small businessmen in particular did not benefit from the 1954 revision. Aimed specifically at small business, however, was a 1958 revision providing for an additional first year write-off deduction of 20 percent of the value of the installed equipment up to $10,000.

The revision of Bulletin F was designed to solve the problems of inadequate depreciation reserves by shortening the useful life of plant and equipment. Thus the original cost of facilities can be recaptured sooner.

All of these enactments tend to help alleviate the problems of inadequate depreciation. However, even current attempts to increase cash flow by increasing depreciation reserves will not be able to make up quickly for the quarter century of underdepreciation which has created the problem for industry.

NOTES

[1] McGraw-Hill Department of Economics, *15th Annual McGraw-Hill Survey of Business Plans for New Plant and Equipment, 1962–1965* (New York, 1962).

[2] *Ibid.*, p. 6.

[3] *Ibid.*, pp. 6–7.

[4] Charles E. Silberman and Todd May, "How Much 'Overcapacity' in U.S. Manufacturing," *Fortune*, September 1958, p. 209.

[5] Burnham Finney, "Can We Prevent a Production Pearl Harbor?" *American Machinist*, July 27, 1959, pp. 89–91.

[6] Two pertinent publications are: George Terborgh, *Realistic Depreciation Policy* (Washington: Machinery & Allied Products Institute, 1954) and George Terborgh, *Business Investment Policy-A MAPI Study and Manual* (Washington: Machinery & Allied Products Institute, 1958).

[7] The Department of Commerce implicit price deflator for structures and equipment purchased by manufacturing establishments shows a similar inflationary trend in recent years. The price deflator for equipment in 1961 stood at 124 percent of its 1954 average.

[8] Machinery and Allied Products Institute, "Underdepreciation From Inflation," *Capital Goods Review*, April 1961, p. 4.

[9] National Industrial Conference Board, *The Economic Almanac*, 1962, p. 93.

[10] McGraw-Hill, Department of Economics, *15th Annual McGraw-Hill Survey of Business Plans for New Plant and Equipment, 1962–1965*, p. 11.

III   *Depreciation and Investment in the Business Firm*

THE MANAGEMENT OF A BUSINESS ENTERPRISE has as one of its principal objectives the profitable investment of available capital resources, or the allocation of capital in the most efficient manner. As a primary source of funds for investment, depreciation is most significant to the operation of the firm. Its significance, however, extends further for depreciation accruals can affect prices, profits and productivity within the firm, and as a result, they are an important consideration in the great majority of managerial decisions. In addition, cash flow, i.e., net earnings plus depreciation, has come into wider acceptance as a gauge of the investment potential of a corporation and is a key element in decisions on mergers or acquisitions.

A higher depreciation rate will increase total cash flow for although it is an additional cost and, consequently, results in a reduction of profits, it also means less in the way of taxes. For example: if a firm adds an additional million dollars to its depreciation cost, presuming a 50 percent tax rate, it will increase its cash flow by $500,000, since the million dollars will go into expenses rather than profits and, consequently, no taxes will be paid on it. If on the other hand the million dollars was allowed to go into profits at a 50 percent tax rate, only $500,000 would remain and thus cash flow would be decreased by $500,000. This increase in cash flow makes it possible to invest more in the business because the depreciation component is increased and the profit component somewhat decreased thus leaving less for dividends and making more available for reinvestment.

It has become customary to define corporate funds according to source

D

as either internal or external; the former is comprised of retained profits and depreciation and the latter includes stocks, bonds, and other debt (i.e., external, long-term capital sources) as well as bank loans and trade payables. Of these sources, both internal and external, depreciation is by far the most extensive. From Table 10 which traces the trend in corporate

TABLE 10

SOURCES OF CORPORATE FUNDS 1949–1964
(billions of dollars)

| Year | Internal Sources | | External Sources | |
	Retained Profits	Depreciation	Long-Term	Short-Term
1949	7.8	7.1	4.3	-3.7
1950	13.0	7.8	4.2	19.2
1951	10.0	9.0	7.8	12.8
1952	7.4	10.4	9.4	3.6
1953	7.9	11.8	7.6	3.1
1954	6.3	13.5	6.4	-4.0
1955	10.9	15.7	8.6	15.1
1956	10.5	17.3	11.1	9.0
1957	9.0	18.7	11.9	2.6
1958	6.0	19.6	10.9	-6.4
1959	9.5	21.6	9.5	16.5
1960	6.2	22.9	9.8	7.4
1961	5.6	24.1	11.8	10.8
1962	7.7	27.5	11.3	12.8
1963	8.0	28.8	10.9	14.8
1964	10.4	30.5	12.7	12.1

Source: Department of Commerce; covers non-financial business corporations; minus sign indicates a reduction in assets or liabilities.

financing from 1949 to 1964, depreciation as a source of funds can be seen to have increased consistently from $7.1 billion in 1949 to $30.5 billion in 1964. By constrast, retained profits, which exceeded depreciation in 1949, stood at $10.4 billion in 1964. This trend reflects the write-off of a larger investment in productive capacity since World War II, the depreciation policies adopted as a result of the Korean War and under the Internal Revenue Code of 1954, as well as the fluctuations which have characterized corporate profits during the postwar period. The preference for internal as opposed to external sources of financing can also be observed.

The significance of depreciation requires that its determination by the business firm be considered. It is an important factor in expenditures for plant and equipment and, further, as one of the costs of production it has an influence on profits and prices. The installation of new plant and equipment involves a major decision for most firms, particularly those engaged in manufacturing for it affects their productivity and, consequently, ability to compete. In the period after World War II, decisions in this area have been made on a more scientific basis than previously and are so intimately tied with a firm's depreciation accrual that they merit discussion here.

To facilitate investment decisions many firms have adopted such procedures as a capital budget and long-range planning committees for capital expenditures. There has also been an attempt on the part of larger firms to stabilize capital expenditures year by year whenever possible and thereby avoid fluctuations in capital investment, which prior to World War II were extremely violent at times.

Investment projects which involve the replacement of existing equipment must be undertaken if the firm is to continue in operation. Others, which involve expansion and the introduction of new products or the replacement of an existing product-line by another, require careful study and investigation to determine whether or not the investment will be made. The criteria used in the decision to accept or reject such projects are many, but for the most part they revolve around profit possibilities and the firm's participation in the market, although the decision to diversify has played a strong role in this matter in recent years.

FACTORS MOTIVATING INVESTMENT DECISIONS

The decision of the firm to invest in plant and equipment may take into account one or more of the following considerations: physical and economic obsolescence, expansion, cost reduction, product improvement and style changes, competitive conditions, capital availability, and the relative cost of equipment rentals.[1]

(1) *Physical and Economic Obsolescence*: Investment may be undertaken by the firm for replacement purposes where the equipment purchased is intended to perform the same function as that which is being discarded or retired. In some instances, the reason for the replacement expenditure is physical deterioration. Wear and tear on a piece of machinery eventually lowers its efficiency and makes it more expensive to operate. Labor and maintenance costs on the machine increase considerably and product quality is affected. Should the new machine be comparable to the old one, the advantage gained from the replacement in kind results from the re-

duction in maintenance costs and improved quality. Very frequently, however, particularly in the case of long-lived equipment, the new machine is technically superior and in such cases some of the profit advantage from the investment results from technological progress. Technology may, in fact, be the principal reason why a replacement investment is undertaken, since the development of new processes and techniques frequently renders machinery economically obsolete. Although a machine in use is operating at near its original efficiency, it may not function favorably on a cost basis compared with its newly developed counterpart. It must be noted that whereas in the long run, rapid progress in production techniques may stimulate investment, in the short run it may cause hesitation for fear that the new machinery will itself soon become economically obsolete.

(2) *Expansion*: It is frequently difficult to distinguish investment for replacement and expansion. In a great many cases, the purchase of capital equipment is undertaken with both objectives in mind. Some plant and equipment expenditures are, however, predominantly expansive in character. Investments related to a marked increase in the demand for a firm's product, to the entrance into a new market or new geographic area, or to the production of a new product are all basically expansive. In such cases, the primary motivation is a decision to increase output or to expand the firm's productive capacity. Replacement often results in a small degree of expansion if the new equipment is more productive than the old.

(3) *Cost Reduction*: Cost reduction is frequently an underlying motive in investments both for replacement and expansion. In the case of replacement, the installation of a new machine that results from retiring some inefficient facility usually offers the firm an opportunity to reduce unit costs in manufacturing operating. Expansion, on the other hand, can reduce costs through the economies involved in larger-scale operations. Cost reduction is desirable primarily because at a given level of sales and prices it results in increased profits. This is particularly significant in the instance of the marginal firm when the profit increase affords the firm an opportunity to sell its goods competitively in order to remain in business. Reduced costs may also make lower prices practical and increase sales where demand is responsive to price changes.

New equipment frequently results in savings on unit labor-costs, whether through increased speed, more automatic operation or process elimination. Increased speed makes more economical use of the operator's time, whereas automatic operations require less manual assistance permitting operators to attend more machines. The elimination of processes by reducing the space needed to perform a given operation effects savings on supervisory personnel. Finally, new equipment cuts labor costs by reducing fatigue and consequent inefficiency.

Modern machinery will often make it possible for a firm to obtain a higher yield on its materials and can also reduce fuel and power requirements per unit of output. It must be stated, however, that in the latter case, power requirements are often greater because of the increased size and speed of operation of the new facility, yet total costs are reduced. The increase in speed often provides for a smoother and more effective flow of materials through the plant and can in many instances reduce the amount of in-process inventory.

(4) *Product Improvement and Style Changes*: Like cost reduction, product improvement and style changes represent possibilities whereby product sales can be increased. The firm might invest in machinery to improve its product either in response to, or in advance of, competitive standards in its industry. The tendency in some industries to spur sales through style obsolescence also affects machinery requirements.

(5) *Competitive Conditions*: The firm's investment policy is affected in varying degrees by the competitive conditions which exist in its industry. A particular investment project may be undertaken precisely because a given facility has been installed by the firm's competition. In some cases, competition may discourage investment by adversely affecting the firm's profit margin and working capital. Competition, on the other hand, may encourage capital expenditures, to gain a larger share of the market but may also delay a proposed investment project if the firm decides that interruption of production to introduce the new facility will reduce its short-run market. In any event, the competitive consequences of an investment project will very likely enter into the firm's decision as to whether or not it will be undertaken.

(6) *Capital Availability*: The firm can invest in plant and equipment only if it has the funds available or can obtain them. As previously noted, a distinction is usually drawn between internal and external sources of capital. Necessary financing must come either from depreciation charges and retained earnings, or by acquiring funds from banks or through the issue of long-term securities. Traditionally the bulk of investment financing in the firm has come from internal sources and in some companies, capital expenditures have been confined completely to funds obtained internally. As a result, the capital that the firm can expect from accumulated depreciation and retained earnings comprises one of the most important considerations motivating decision to invest.

The preference for an aversion to internal capital sources as opposed to external sources can be either a matter of choice or one of necessity, depending upon the firm's financial status and the conditions which prevail in the capital markets. Some of the larger or more prosperous firms oppose external financing not because of any problem in acquiring outside funds but simply because they prefer not to finance externally. Dean offers a reason why this is so:

> ... debt financing for venture purposes cramps management's style. Most bank loans and bonds carry restrictions on the uses to be made of money, on future financing, on minimum levels of certain balance sheet items, and on dividend payments. They further put a fixed capital cost on the firm, since a periodic cash outlay sometimes extends into the unknown future, regardless of conditions or opportunities. Preferred stock ... is not ... much better in this respect. Furthermore, debt lowers the credit standing of the firm.[2]

Some firms which are either relatively small or marginal producers in their respective industries do not finance from external sources since it is often difficult for them to acquire outside funds on favorable terms. In such instances the lack of capital will act as a major deterrent to investment. Where depreciation exists as the major source of capital, accruals which are inadequate even for replacement purposes place a curb on investment which is even more severe.

A policy of accelerated depreciation such as existed during World War II and was later revived in the Korean crisis has a definite effect on the availability of capital for investment. In firms where depreciation charges comprise a significant percentage of the capital resources available for investment, accelerated depreciation should act as a stimulus to investment. Further, it has the advantage of mitigating the problem of obsolescence and to some extent inflation since it allows investment to be recouped more rapidly and thus reduces the risk in capital expenditure. Capital availability can be affected by a change in tax policy and within recent years has, in fact, been affected by such a change.

A liberalization of the depreciation-tax laws is most useful to those firms for which depreciation constitutes a large portion of total cost. These are capital intensive firms, and depreciation-tax changes most definitely have a very different impact upon them than upon firms which are labor intensive. In addition, provision for increased depreciation allowances is most useful to those firms which can offset such increases against taxable income. A firm with a relatively small tax base may not be able to take advantage of the revision.

(7) *Equipment Rentals*: In its investment decision the firm frequently has to decide whether to purchase a particular capital good outright or to acquire its services through rental.[3] In either case the advantage to be gained from the use of the facility would be the same. The firm's decision,

therefore, will be based primarily on the relative costs involved in the two alternatives. Other considerations, however, may enter its decision. For example, where debt financing is necessary for purchase, its implications for the firm's credit standing and balance sheet give asset rental added attraction, since in leaseholds neither the asset nor the liability is entered on the balance sheet.[4]

PRODUCTIVITY

Depreciation is a cost of production and also provides the means for renewing capital equipment. Thus it can and does affect productivity, profits and, in some cases, prices. In those instances where charges for depreciation do not provide fully for the capital consumed, a series of price, profit and productivity considerations can arise which may affect business adversely. This is particularly true in periods of inflation and rapid technological change. During these times write-off rates on relatively long-lived equipment (i.e., ten to fifteen years) will fall short of covering capital consumption costs unless some provision is made for price-level changes and rapid obsolescence. All firms in an industry are affected regardless of size. However, smaller firms and marginal producers will be affected most severely. In many cases these have only limited access to capital markets and cannot readily obtain financing to provide for the excess of replacement costs over depreciation accruals.

Where depreciation accruals do not provide for capital costs, the firm will often find it necessary to postpone much-needed plant and equipment replacements. In such a manner, by forcing continued operation of technically or physically inferior equipment, inadequate accruals generate and prolong obsolescence. This has a decided effect on the rate of productivity in the firm. Further, insofar as the problem of capital renewal and depreciation is common to industry in general, the national rate of productivity increase is likewise affected.

In many segments of American industry improved plant and equipment is a requisite for increased productivity. Other causes of greater output per man-hour and output per dollar of investment, such as improved practices, incentive plans, and the beneficiation of raw materials, are significant but have their limitations. In fact, raw material beneficiation can only be accomplished in most instances by the installation of capital equipment. This is typified by the sintering plants used in the steel industry and the washing plants in the coal industry.

Because of the significance of capital investment, the replacement of obsolete equipment almost invariably results in productivity increases as well as greater overall production. An example taken from the steel industry serves to demonstrate this tendency: A mill for rolling cold reduced steel sheets, installed in 1935, had a speed of 3,000 to 4,000 feet per minute; its present-day counterpart is rated at between 5,000 and 6,000 feet per minute. In this instance, the replacement is operated with the same crew and runs at a much higher rate than the old mill, providing an increase not only in man-hour output but also capacity.

The emphasis placed on productivity raises the question of its importance. Productivity is the principal means available for increasing the nation's wealth. It is a ratio between the input factors of production, namely, manpower, raw materials and capital equipment, and the resultant output. Increases in product per man-hour, per unit of raw materials and per machine actually increase total wealth. Further, increased productivity strengthen the ability of industries to compete with foreign producers. Competition from abroad, although not an overwhelming problem for the entire economy, is serious for some industries. With industrial development growing rapidly in Japan and the expansion of productive capacity in the Common Market, foreign competition will continue to increase. Both the European countries and the Japanese have a high degree of modern equipment which produces a quality product. When this is coupled with the fact that wage rates are much lower than those in the United States, it can be readily seen that we face formidable competition. Thus it is evident that we must use the means at our disposal to meet this competition, and one such means is increasing productivity.

DEPRECIATION WRITE-OFFS AND PROFITS

If depreciation reserves do not account fully for the cost of capital erosion, total costs before taxes cannot be recorded, and as a result, the firm's after-tax profits are overstated. This situation occurs most frequently in those industries and firms which employ large aggregates of heavy, long-lived equipment. The experience of one firm will serve to illustrate this condition: the company purchased a depreciable facility in 1939 at an approximate cost of $1 million. The life of the asset was 20 years so that on a straight-line basis, 5 percent or $50,000 was to be written off each year. However, owing to price-level changes, $50,000 in 1958, the last year of the asset's life, was the equivalent of approximately $25,000 in 1939. From the standpoint of constant dollar value, therefore, only 2.5 percent was written off in 1958. To achieve a 5 percent write-off, some $100,000, the actual cost of capital consumption, should have been charged to depreciation. This was not permissible, so that actual capital costs in the amount of $50,000 were credited to pre-tax profits. With an income tax rate of 52 percent, profits in this case were inflated by approximately $25,000. When the excess of replacement costs over depreciation accruals is drawn from profits, the overstatement amounts to $50,000, since this amount is used to cover cost and is not available to perform the profit function.

The 1957 Annual Report of the Indiana Telephone Company exemplified the overstatement of profits under inadequate depreciation accruals. Both the balance sheet and profit and loss statement contained an additional column to demonstrate the effects of inflation. To indicate the value of the company's plant in current dollars, the figure under the classification "net plant" was increased from $6,935,615.69 to $8,572,366.95. If the tax law had contained a provision for price-level changes, the company would have added an additional $1,636,751.26 to its balance sheet. Similarly, in the profit and loss statement the total depreciation taken was $355,652, whereas actual capital erosion was $469,797, about $114,000, or one-third more. It was then indicated that profits, which were stated at $317,846, were actually $203,207 when account was taken of real depreciation costs. The substantial overstatement of profits derived from the use of almost a third of net income after taxes for replacement purposes to make up the depreciation deficiency.[5]

Another instance of the overstatement of profits was developed by Jones in a study on the effect of price level changes on financial statements. In considering the question of depreciation he stated:

The point at which price-level changes are apt to have the greatest impact upon income statement is the depreciation of plant and equipment. The assets have been purchased at various levels in the past, often when the value of the dollar was much greater than it is today. As a result, the depreciation charge is a combination of costs incurred at various price levels and does not reflect the cost of plant and equipment at the current or any other uniform value of the dollar.[6]

In support of this statement figures were offered on a company which indicated that over a twelve-year period from 1940 to 1951 only $3,315,000 in depreciation costs were permitted, whereas $4,033,000 represented the actual cost of wear and tear on the company's facilities. The years examined included (1) the period when rapid amortization was allowed during the war; and (2) a higher total depreciation figure after 1949 by virtue of a merger with a foreign affiliate. In 1947 and 1948, before the merger occurred, the deficit between what was actually written off and what should have been ($63,000 and $75,000 respectively) was 28 percent. Profits were inflated by this much each year.[7]

In regard to the economic system in general, estimates were made on the total overstatement of profits. One economist placed the figure for the 1947–1956 decade at $44 billion. It was estimated in 1959 that the overstatement of profit was approximately $6 billion per year.[8] This was understandable in view of the fact that in large industries, such as the utilities and steel, the phantom profit which derived from insufficient depreciation reached several hundred million dollars per year.

DEPRECIATION AND PRICES

One of the principal objectives of the business firm is to have income which will cover all its costs. Where capital costs are not fully accounted for through depreciation charges before taxes, provision for the excess cost of plant replacement must be made from some other source. As has been indicated, this is frequently done from profits with the result that they are actually overstated. This entire situation can in some instances have an effect on the pricing policy of the firm, particularly in a seller's market. It is true that prices are very often determined by factors beyond the firm's control: possible competition from other firms in the industry and the availability of substitute materials. However, in a seller's market such as existed after World War II there is a tendency for firms to price their product in such a way as to cover all costs. If the cost of wear and tear on capital equipment is not cared for before taxes and must be taken in part out of profits, it is necessary for the firm to earn more profits after taxes as a supplement to depreciation. This requires a greater gross income before taxes and, consequently, the possibility of higher prices. In a buyer's market, there is rarely such a possibility because competitive forces will keep prices down. It is only in a seller's market that inadequate depreciation accruals can have an effect on prices, and give them an upward bias.

NOTES

[1] Motivational factors involved in the decision to invest are discussed in Ruth Mack, *The Flow of Business Funds and Consumer Purchasing Power* (New York, Columbia University Press, 1941), pp. 242–259; Joel Dean, *Managerial Economics* (New York, Prentice-Hall, 1951), pp. 603–608; Walter W. Heller, "The Anatomy of Investment Decisions," *Harvard Business Review*, 29, No. 2 (March, 1951), pp. 99–101.

[2] Joel Dean, *Managerial Economics* (New York, Prentice-Hall, 1951), pp. 580–581.

[3] This consideration is more common to small firms.

[4] See Dean, *op cit.*, p. 581 and Joseph D. Coppock, *Economics of the Business Firm* (New York, McGraw-Hill, 1959), pp. 333–334. In addition to the reasons for investment discussed here, decisions of the firm to act or not act on an

expenditure proposal may be governed by a number of irrational elements or psychological factors; see Mack, *op. cit.* (n. 1, above), pp. 268–271.

[5] Indiana Telephone Company, *Annual Report to Stockholders*, December 31, 1957, pp. 6–7.

[6] Ralph Coughenour Jones, *Price Level Changes and Financial Statements: Case Studies of Four Companies* (American Accounting Association, 1955), pp. 120–121.

[7] *Ibid.*, p. 121.

[8] William A. Paton, "Insufficient Depreciation: What It Does to the Economy," *Current Business Studies*, Society of Business Advisory Professions, Number 32–33, p. 33.

IV *Depreciation Practices in Foreign Countries*

AN EXAMINATION OF THE TAX PROVISIONS relating to depreciation in the industrialized countries of Europe and in Japan is most revealing.[1] The differential in tax laws, particularly marked prior to 1962, has contributed significantly to the growth of foreign competition and the flow of investment capital from the United States. This differential can be observed in Table 11 which compares the deductions for depreciation in the United States with those allowed in leading industrialized countries abroad.

Prior to the revenue revision in 1962 the margin of disadvantage facing United States producers via depreciation write-offs was considerable. On the average, the rate of recovery on investments in new industrial equipment during the first year of its use was more than twice as rapid in the nine foreign countries considered than in the United States. The foreign countries recovered 29 percent of the total investment during the first year, while the allowable recovery in this country was limited to only 13.3 percent. In relation to the United Kingdom (39 percent) and Japan (43.4 percent) our first-year disadvantage was much more severe. In 1962, with the new depreciation guidelines and the 7 per cent investment credit, the first-year recovery rate in the United States was brought into line with the nine-country average. This, however, is not the case with recovery rates during subsequent years.

During the first two years in which industrial equipment is operative, industries in the United States may now recover 42.5 percent of their original investment. This is a significant improvement over the pre-1962

TABLE 11

DEPRECIATION DEDUCTIONS, INITIAL AND INVESTMENT ALLOWANCES*
FOR INDUSTRIAL EQUIPMENT IN FOREIGN INDUSTRIAL COUNTRIES AND
SIMILAR DEDUCTIONS AND ALLOWANCES IN THE UNITED STATES

	Representative Tax Lives in Years	*Depreciation Deductions, Initial and Investment Allowances (percentage of cost of asset)*		
		1st year	*1st 2 years*	*1st 5 years*
Belgium	8	22.5	45.0	92.5
Canada	10	30.0	44.0	71.4
France	10	25.0	43.8	76.3
West Germany	10	20.0	36.0	67.2
Italy	10	25.0	50.0	100.0
Japan	16	43.4	51.0	68.2
Netherlands	10	26.2	49.6	85.6
Sweden	5	30.0	51.0	100.0
United Kingdom	27	39.0	46.3	64.0
Average, 9 foreign countries†		29.0	46.3	80.6
United States:				
Practice prior to July 11, 1962	15	13.3	24.9	51.1
With new depreciation guidelines	12	16.7	30.6	59.8
With new depreciation guidelines and investment credit (7%)‡	12	29.5	42.5	69.6

* The deductions and allowances for each of the foreign countries were computed on the assumption that the investment qualifies fully for any special allowances or deductions permitted. The deductions in the United States were determined using the double-declining balance depreciation method, without regard to the limited first-year allowances for small business.

† The average figures for the nine foreign countries represent unweighted arithmetic averages, as sufficient data were not readily available to permit the computation of a weighted and more meaningful average.

‡ The 7 percent investment credit has been considered as equivalent to a 14 percent investment allowance for the purpose of this table.

Source: Prepared by the Office of Financial Analysis, U.S. Treasury Department and contained in "State of the Economy and Policies for Full Employment," *Hearings before the Joint Economic Committee Congress of the United States,* 87th Congress, 2nd Session, August 17, 1962, p. 670.

allowable recovery of 24.9 percent, but it is still below the nine-country average of 46.3 percent. When the recovery on investment during the first five years of an asset's use is considered, the depreciation-tax changes of 1962 are seen to be even less effective in reducing the margin of disadvantage. Although the allowable rate of recovery during the five-year period has been increased from 51.1 to 69.6 percent, this is still 11 percent

TABLE 12

MAXIMUM CORPORATE INCOME TAX RATES IN FOREIGN
INDUSTRIAL COUNTRIES AND IN THE UNITED STATES

	Tax Rate (percent)
Belgium	30.00
Canada	50.00
France	50.00
West Germany	51.00
Italy	40.00*
Japan	38.00
Netherlands	44.00†
Sweden	40.00
United Kingdom	53.75
Average, 9 Foreign Countries:	44.08
United States:	50.00

* A precise total rate for corporate income tax in Italy is not possible because of the complexity and variations in the tax structure. In general, the maximum central government rate may be said to be approximately 40 percent.

† In the Netherlands taxable profits under fl. 40,000 are taxed at the 44 percent rate. For taxable profits between fl. 40,000 and fl. 50,000 the tax rate is 44 percent plus a 15 percent surtax on the amount over fl. 40,000. Taxable profit above fl. 50,000 is taxed at a 47 percent rate.

below the nine-country average of 80.6 percent. In relation to specific countries, namely, Belgium, Italy, the Netherlands, and Sweden, the spread is more pronounced. In Italy and Sweden, for example, 100 percent of the cost of an asset may be written off during the first five years of its use.

Therefore, even with the introduction of the new depreciation guidelines and the 7 percent investment credit, the treatment accorded new investment in this country is not as favorable as in other leading industrialized nations. Consequently, our foreign competitors maintain a reduced but significant advantage where depreciation write-offs are concerned.

To lend more meaning to the discussion of depreciation tax laws abroad, and for the purposes of comparison, it will be helpful to state the maximum corporate income rates for the nine industrialized nations under discussion. This is done in Table 12, the average rate for the nine foreign nations being 44.08 percent as compared with a 50 percent rate in the United States.

COMPARISON OF TAX DEPRECIATION SYSTEMS

The comparison of international tax depreciation systems is an involved procedure for the variations found within the systems are many. Programs differ in their write-off methods, life estimates, asset classifications, accounting procedures, etc. Basically, however, the tax laws in a great number of foreign countries provide for three things: (1) revaluation of assets to correct for the erosion of capital due to inflation; (2) flexibility in determining the useful life of an asset; (3) some incentive or allowance to encourage investment. This will become apparent in the review of foreign depreciation programs which follows. In all some thirty countries are included, among them the industrialized nations referred to above, as well as the Latin American and African nations.

Canada

The Canadian system of depreciation allowances is of particular interest since the Canadian economy so closely parallels that of the United States. Further, Canada has been a proving ground for experiments with depreciation policy as a means of stimulating economic activity and foreign trade.

The straight-line method of depreciation was in effect up to 1939, with some extra allowances conceded for abnormal use. At that time, with the economy in the doldrums, a new policy was instituted as a stimulant, whereby an additional allowance of 10 percent was alloted on new capital expenditures.[2] The advent of the war resulted in the introduction of increased flexibility in the Canadian code, as was the case in other countries, and resistance developed to a reversion to more stringent policies. Further liberalization was introduced at this time as a result of the strain which developed on Canadian dollar resources. Among the measures taken by the Government to stimulate exports was the acceleration of depreciation on plant and other assets used in the production of commodities for export. Depreciation at double the normal rates was granted on new assets in specific categories. This policy was initiated in 1944 and due to its success was extended until 1949.

The current method of computing depreciation was introduced with the 1949 liberalization. The Capital Cost Allowance presented a new approach in writing off expenditures on fixed assets. Its liberality is found in its main feature, the treatment of useful lives under a "bracket system" of optional annual allowances based on maximum-minimum rates of charge-off applicable to the diminishing values of depreciable property. With the exception of certain farmers or fishermen who are allowed to use the straight-line method, all taxpayers must compute depreciation using the diminishing or declining-balance method of write-off. Depreciable assets are grouped into specified classes or "brackets," and depreciation is computed with respect to each class as a whole rather than for individual assets. Deductions on particular assets may vary from year to year within the scope of the bracket so long as a maximum limit is observed. Some of the property classes which have been established are of general application (e.g. buildings) whereas others specify particular types of industrial equipment (e.g. electrical generating equipment, pulp and paper machinery). Because of the numerical limitation of categories (there are 14), most machinery and equipment falls into the "all other" class (class 8). It is chiefly in the "bracket system" that the liberal nature of Canadian policy is to be found, since the Canadian code makes no provision for specific incentive allowances or for adjustments to price-level changes.

In order to clarify the bracket system more fully a listing of each of the 14 categories, with limited examples of assets contained in each of them, and the maximum allowable rate of depreciation for each using the declining-balance method is presented in Table 13. It should be noted that in the vast majority of instances the rates were more liberal than those provided in the United States prior to the Bulletin F revision in 1962. For example, on general machinery the taxpayer in Canada may write off up to 20 percent of cost, whereas 10 percent was the maximum rate in the United States. In general, the Canadian system permitted depreciation at up to twice the United States rate. A substantial difference was found in the rate assigned to a fundamental asset, machine tools. A 20 percent write-off is granted in Canada, whereas the United States rate was merely 6 percent. The new rates introduced under "Revenue Procedure 62–21" have improved our relative position.

The rates assigned to the various classes of depreciable assets may be modified upward in the case of an individual taxpayer upon petition to the Internal Revenue Service. Further, the Canadian law allows for any

E

amount less than the maximum rate to be written off in any one year. The taxpayer may vary the rate from year to year, as long as he observes

TABLE 13

RATES OF DEPRECIATION ON CLASSES OF DEPRECIABLE ASSETS SPECIFIED
UNDER THE CANADIAN BRACKET SYSTEM

Category*	Example of Assets in Each Class	Depreciation Rate†
Class 1	Bridges; canals, dams; surface construction, e.g., roads, sidewalks	4%
Class 2	Electrical generating equipment, oil, gas and water pipelines; gas and electric distributing equipment	6
Class 3	Building or other structures	5
Class 4	Railway systems; trolley or bus systems or tramways	6
Class 5	Pulp and paper mills	10
Class 6	Tank cars; temporary structures	10
Class 7	Ships, scows; marine railways	15
Class 8‡	Tangible capital assets not included in another class; includes most machinery and equipment	20
Class 9	Radio transmitting and receiving equipment; radar equipment	25
Class 10	Automotive equipment; mining machinery; building contractor's movable equipment	30
Class 11	Neon signs, electrical advertising signs	35
Class 12	Library books; chinaware, cutlery	100
Class 16	Aircraft furniture or fittings attached to an aircraft	40
Class 17	Telephone and telegraph equipment	8

* A taxpayer may elect to include under Class 1 all properties which would otherwise be included in another class. A taxpayer whose chief depreciable assets are in Class 2, 4 or 17, may elect that any other property from the same business be included in Class 2, 4 or 17.

† Depreciation rate figured using declining-balance method.

‡ Class 8, which represents the "all other" category with a rate of 20 percent, is most significant since it includes the great part of machinery and equipment in general use commercially and in factories.

Source: C. C. H. Canadian Ltd., *Canadian Master Tax Guide*, 15th edition, 1960.

the maximum ceiling. By taking advantage of this provision, the taxpayer need not waste high write-offs during periods of declining business and income; they may be accumulated to be applied in good years. This acknowledgment of varied levels of earnings imparts needed flexibility to the system.

In 1961 the Canadian Parliament initiated a temporary measure to liberalize the system further. The Double Depreciation Program entitles firms to claim double the normal annual depreciation formerly allowed on assets acquired after December 1960 for the production of new products. The ruling applies to products not ordinarily or previously manufactured in Canada and to those which have been manufactured there, but in areas of surplus manpower. It has been projected that $350 million worth of new industry will qualify for deductions under the incentive program.[3]

Accelerated depreciation was introduced as a part of the 1961 budget proposal. It purpose is to stimulate re-equipment and modernization and thus assist Canadian industry to become more competitive in markets at home and abroad. The re-equipment and modernization allowance provides a 50 percent increase in the rate of depreciation claimable during the first year of an asset's useful life. For example, an allowance rate of 30 percent instead of the normal 20 percent is deductible the first year for equipment in Class 8, the "all other" category. Additions qualifying for the allowance are those in excess of a normal level of expansion or a certain base amount. The base is the aggregate of the amounts spent on depreciable property acquired in the last complete taxation year, or the average of the last three taxation years, whichever is greater. The additional allowance applies to new assets acquired in the period June 21, 1961 to March 31, 1963. Practically all assets depreciable on a declining-balance basis are eligible for the additional allowance. Assets already being depreciated on an accelerated basis under certificates from the Minister of Defense Production and property already eligible for a 100 percent rate of depreciation do not qualify.[4]

Questions have arisen concerning the loss of revenue incurred by the government through the enactment of these liberal depreciation provisions. A study of Canadian corporate profits, taxes, depreciation and capital formation tends to disprove the claim that corporate income taxes would decrease proportionally to the increase in depreciation.[5] The report asserts that even though depreciation increased to 63.7 percent of corporate profits before taxes in 1959, the Government was able to reduce the effective tax rate to 43.9 percent. The 1952 rate was 51.3 percent and depreciation was 44.1 percent of corporate profits before taxes. Likewise, the amount of capital formation began an upward trend about the same time the liberalization of depreciation occurred. Thus the Canadian experience sustains the conclusion that liberalized depreciation allowances do not impair revenues.

United Kingdom

Similar to the Canadian code, the tax law in the United Kingdom makes no provision for a revaluation of assets, and in that respect it is perhaps more stringent than those of other major European industrial countries. On the Continent, only the Scandinavian countries and Switzerland did not make any provision for revaluation after the war.

The various classes of assets to which depreciation allowances can be applied were established through the enactment of successive statutes beginning with the Finance Act of 1919. The major modifications of the depreciation laws were embodied in the Income Tax Act of 1952 and subsequent legislation in the Finance Acts of 1952, 1953, 1954, and 1956.

Depreciation in the United Kingdom is regarded in a different light from most countries. It is not treated as an expense deduction in computing net business profits, but is deducted from the amount of net profits assessed. As a result, special adjustments are required to preserve the benefit of unused depreciation in the event of business losses.[6]

Three methods of computing the depreciation allowances may be employed: declining-balance, which is the most commonly used method; straight-line, the alternative approach; and thirdly, a special method which applies to the mineral extractive industries. Industrial buildings and structures must be depreciated on a straight-line basis.

The law of the U.K. now has annual rates of 15, 20, and 25 percent on a declining-balance method, depending on the length of life of the asset. Assets with an expected life of 18 years or more, such as furniture and fittings, have a declining balance rate of 15 percent or a fixed annual rate of $6\frac{1}{4}$ percent. For machinery and equipment with an expected life of 14–18 years, the declining-balance rate is 20 percent or $8\frac{1}{2}$ percent on a fixed annual rate. For motor vehicles and equipment with a life of less than 14 years, the declining balance rate is 25 percent or $11\frac{1}{4}$ percent on a fixed annual basis.

The tax law in the United Kingdom is particularly liberal in the establishment of additional attractions for investment in plant and equipment. It permits investment allowances and initial allowances which can be considered a form of accelerated depreciation. Both incentives provide for deductions on the acquisition of a number of types of depreciable assets. For most types of industrial equipment the investment allowance is 20 percent, whereas the initial allowance is 10 percent. Both are in addition to the regular depreciation allowed during the first year. They differ in that the initial allowance reduces depreciation costs or the basic value of the asset upon which subsequent years' depreciation is figured, whereas the investment allowance does not so reduce depreciation costs. Since the investment allowance is in addition to regular depreciation and an initial allowance and does not reduce the basis for computing subsequent years' depreciation, taxpayers are able to deduct more than 100 percent of the cost of an asset over its useful life. The rates of the investment allowance range from 10 percent on industrial buildings to 40 percent on ships, with 20 percent the rate for most types of industrial equipment. Consequently, taxpayers can deduct 120 percent of the cost of industrial equipment over the period of depreciation, and amounts ranging from 110 percent to 140 percent on other depreciable assets. If, for example, one purchased an item of industrial equipment for $100,000, he could take an investment allowance of $20,000; an initial allowance

TABLE 14

INITIAL ALLOWANCE RATES IN THE UNITED KINGDOM
(IN PERCENT)

	Machinery and Equipment	Industrial Buildings
April 6, 1946, to April 5, 1949	20	10
April 6, 1949, to April 5, 1952	40	10
April 6, 1952, to April 14, 1953	0	0
April 15, 1953, to April 14, 1958	20	10
April 15, 1958, to April 7, 1959	30	10
Current Rate	10	5

Source: *Treasury Memorandum on Foreign Depreciation Systems,* p. 719.

of $10,000, plus ordinary depreciation of $10,000, if the asset had a ten year life. If he chooses to use the declining-balance method with a surcharge, the 10 percent of normal depreciation would be increased in the first year to 12.5 percent. Consequently, 42.5 percent of the asset's value could be written off in the first year. Further, the base for the second year would be 77.5 per cent of the asset's value since the 20 percent investment allowance is not deducted from it.

Initial allowances were first introduced in the United Kingdom in 1946, and since that time the rates of allowance have been changed on a number of occasions, as is evident from Table 14 below. The current rates apply to expenditures made after April 7, 1959. They range from 5 percent on industrial buildings and structures to 30 percent on automobiles and used assets, including ships and cars. As already noted, the initial allowance rate for most types of industrial equipment is 10 percent.

Investment allowances, not to be confused with initial allowances, were first introduced in 1954, and since that time several rate changes have been made. Between April 6, 1954, and February 17, 1956, the rate was 20 percent on both industrial buildings and industrial machinery and equipment. From February 18, 1956, to April 7, 1959, investment allowances were suspended after which time current rates were introduced (i.e. 20 percent on industrial machinery and 10 percent on industrial buildings). Prior to April 7, 1959, an investment allowance and an initial allowance could not be claimed on the same asset. For assets acquired after that date, both allowances may be claimed.

Under the tax law, scientific research facilities receive special treatment. Capital expenditures for scientific research may be written off at a rate of 60 percent during the first year and a 10 percent write-off is permitted in each of the next four years as a deductible business expense. Such assets also qualify for an investment allowance of 20 percent so that 80 percent of the total investment is deductible in the first year with a total recovery of 120 percent. No initial deduction is allowable.

Provisions have been made for the application of balancing charges and balancing deductions in the case of depreciable assets. Balancing deductions stem from a recognition that the depreciation allowed has been less than that which has actually taken place. Therefore, additional depreciation is allowed in the year of an asset's disposition in order to take into account the excess of depreciation cost over that claimed. On the other hand, balancing charges acknowledge the fact that the depreciation allowed has been excessive. The amount added to the assessment for the year in which the capital asset is sold represents the excess of the amount realized over depreciated cost.

On the question of unused depreciation, if the depreciation deductions cannot be fully obtained during any tax year due to an insufficiency of taxable profits, any unused depreciation may be added to the amount available for subsequent years. It may be accumulated from year to year without limitation until full benefit is obtained.

France

France has a liberal system of depreciation for tax purposes in a number of respects. Schedules for the determination of asset lives have been kept flexible, provision has been made for accelerated depreciation and steps have been taken to compensate for the effects of price-level changes: however, no incentive allowances are provided.

With a high rate of inflation endured during the postwar period, a system of asset revaluation was provided from 1945 through 1958 on the basis of inflation coefficients and stipulated that in no event could price changes occurring after June 30, 1959, be taken into account. Taxpayers were given until 1962 to complete the revaluation process. This final revaluation was mandatory for enterprises with profits in excess of 5 million francs (new). The 1959 readjustment of inflation coefficients is as in Table 15.

The revaluation was made by multiplying the original cost of the asset by the stipulated coefficient for the year in which it was acquired. Past depreciation charges were also revalued by the same set of factors so that the remaining life or net depreciable property was determined by

TABLE 15

FRANCE: 1959 ADJUSTMENT OF INFLATION COEFFICIENTS

Year of Acquisition of Asset	Coefficient Used Prior to 1959 Tax Reform	Coefficient Used After the 1959 Tax Reform
1914 or earlier	204.1	243.0
1924	43.5	51.8
1934	54.4	64.8
1944	13.7	16.3
1954	1.15	1.25
1955	1.15	1.25
1956	1.10	1.20
1957	1.05	1.15
1958	1.00	1.05

subtracting one adjusted figure from the other. A revaluation reserve was then set up upon which a 3 percent tax was levied. The payment of this tax freed the funds to be used for any other purpose.

The straight-line method of computing depreciation deductions was used for assets acquired before December 31, 1959. The declining-balance method became mandatory for assets acquired after January 1, 1965. For assets acquired between these two dates, the taxpayer may apply the declining-balance method if his asset qualifies, or may continue to use the straight-line method. The same system, however, must be applied to all assets acquired during this period to which the election applies. Should the declining-balance method be chosen, the special acceleration provisions made in the French law may not be used; under the straight-line method they remain in effect. All industrial machinery and equipment having a useful life in excess of three years can be depreciated according to the declining-balance method.

Rates of depreciation have been kept flexible and may be negotiated either by individual taxpayers or industrial groups. Plants and machinery are allowed an annual write-off of from 7 to 15 percent. However, for the most part, machinery is written off at 15 percent, or in a seven-year span. This period can be decreased to five or three and one-half years if the machinery is used in multiple shift operations. Heavy machinery is usually written off in ten years.

Under the declining-balance system, straight-line rates may be increased by 1.5 for property with a life of 3 or 4 years, doubled for assets having a life of 5 or 6 years, and increased by 2.5 times for assets with lives of more than 6 years. Where the declining-balance method is being used, the taxpayer may switch to the straight-line method when the stage is reached at which the straight-line deduction exceeds that which results from the declining-balance system.

As has been noted, there are provisions in the law for accelerated depreciation. New plant, equipment, and tools acquired after December 31, 1951 which have a normal useful life of over five years may be written off at double depreciation for the first year. Depreciation is computed in the ordinary manner and two annual deductions are taken in the first year. This reduces the period of depreciation by one year.

An additional allowance of 10 percent during the first year is permitted for plant and equipment acquired for modernization. If this allowance is taken, other deductions for depreciation are made on the basis of 90 percent of cost. If the item of equipment qualifies, both the initial allowance of 10 percent and double depreciation can be taken during the first year.

In order to improve her competitive position in the production of steel and coal, France has permitted these industries additional depreciation deductions based on the volume of turnover or sales. Normal depreciation is used as the minimum limit, and a maximum is established as a percentage of gross sales. This percentage varies from product to product, e.g., 8 percent of the sales of Bessemer steel, 20 percent of iron ore sales and 4 percent for ferro-manganese. The difference between this maximum and minimum constitutes an optional deduction. If, for example, normal depreciation is 1,000,000 francs but the maximum computed according to sales is 1,500,000 francs, the taxpayer has the option to take 500,000 francs as a tax deduction and apply it to any depreciable asset he owns.

In 1958, France permitted added depreciation for the cost of assets used in scientific and technical research, i.e., an additional 50 percent deduction was allowed for the first year. The balance was to be written off over the useful life of the asset. The application of this concession was limited to assets acquired prior to January 1, 1960.

In 1957, a special "export" depreciation deduction was granted to encourage exports. The deduction is calculated by multiplying the year's normal depreciation allowance by the ratio of the firm's sales for export to total sales volume for the year. In 1959, the export deduction was increased by 50 percent.

Unclaimed portions of allowable deductions for depreciation as a result of business losses may be passed on to subsequent years. If the depreciation is not claimed due to the fact that it was not recorded on the books, this depreciation is not carried forward but is used to increase the life of the asset.

West Germany

In West Germany rates of depreciation have been kept flexible and provision is made for accelerated write-offs. Adjustments for price-level changes are not currently allowed, although revaluation was permitted on assets acquired prior to June 21, 1948, on the basis of August 1948 replacement costs and subsequent write-offs are calculated on the basis of this revaluation. West Germany currently makes no provision for incentive allowances.

To depreciate movable assets either the straight-line or declining-balance method may be used. Buildings, however, must be depreciated according to the straight-line method. Depreciation rates are determined through negotiation with individual taxpayers and are based on the expected economic life of particular assets under the conditions that exist in individual businesses. Account is also taken of extraordinary wear and tear as well as technological obsolescence. If the declining-balance is used, the rates are twice the straight-line rates, but in no case may they exceed 20 percent of the asset's value for one year. Table 16 presents some typical useful lives and declining-balance rates of depreciation. For machinery and equipment used in operations that require double or triple shifts, depreciation rates may be increased by 25 to 50 percent.

The tax law contains a number of provisions for accelerated depreciation. Basic industries such as coal, iron, and steel, etc., may write off 50 percent of their movable assets and 30 percent of fixed assets during the first five years. Enterprises located close to the border of the Iron Curtain may write off 50 percent of the cost of movable assets and 30 percent of the cost of fixed assets in the first two years. All investment in Berlin receives accelerated allowances. Up to 75 percent of the cost of movable assets may be recovered in the first three years provided such assets remain in Berlin for an additional three-year period. Special accelerated allowances have been introduced as an incentive for private hospital construction, for the low-income groups, for equipment and properties used to control sewage and waste, and for movable assets for air pollution control.

Although currently the tax law makes no provision for initial or investment allowances a number of such incentives were in effect after 1948.

TABLE 16

WEST GERMANY: TYPICAL USEFUL LIVES AND DECLINING-BALANCE RATES
OF DEPRECIATION

Type of Machinery and Equipment	Estimated Life in Years	Declining-Balance Rates of Depreciation
Iron and Steel Industry:		
Blast Furnace	10	20%
Open Hearth Furnace	10	20
Electric Furnace	10	20
Automobile Industry:		
Boring and Turning Mills	2–5	20
Radial Drills	10	20
Engine Lathe (automatic)	6	20
Hydraulic Press	8	20
Textile Industry:		
Carding Machines	10	20
Combers	12	16
Looms (single)	12–15	13–16
Knitting Machines	8–12	16–20

Source: *Treasury Memorandum on Foreign Depreciation Systems*, p. 707.

They were allowed in addition to regular depreciation during the early years of useful life, but the total write-off was never allowed to exceed the cost of the asset. Such initial incentive devices, one author claims, were originally proposed by the German Government not as devices to stimulate recovery, but as instruments for the evasion of tax policies imposed by the Occupation Powers.[7] A steeply graduated tax structure had been introduced by the Allied Control Council in 1946 and these incentives, it was said, served to eliminate much of the impact of the tax. It is further brought out that the incentive measures not only directly stimulated savings and investment but were indirectly anti-inflationary insofar as they curtailed private consumption.

Italy

The tax law in Italy requires that depreciation be computed on a straight-line basis; however, provision is made for accelerated depreciation. The law currently does not allow asset revaluation, although in 1953 all pre-1948 assets were revalued by a system of coefficients reflecting the degree of inflation. Subsequent deductions for depreciation are figured on the basis of this revaluation. No provision is made for initial or investment allowances.

Rates of depreciation under the Italian law are flexible since they are

TABLE 17

ITALY: ANNUAL RATES OF DEPRECIATION

Nature of Asset	Percentage per Annum
Industrial Buildings	3
Installations for General Services and Internal Transport and Handling of Merchandise	6
Machinery	12
Equipment	10
Fittings	15
Furniture and Office Machines	10
Automotive Equipment	20

Source: Price, Waterhouse & Company, *Information Guide for Those Doing Business in Italy*, January 1963, p. 16.

established for broad groups of assets rather than for specific pieces of equipment. Current rates were established on March 1, 1957, by the Italian Minister of Finance and an extensive list was provided of annual rates of depreciation for fixed assets of most industrial and commercial enterprises. Furnaces in the steel industry, for example, are depreciated at 10 percent and agricultural buildings at 3 percent. The rates allowed in the case of firms not specifically listed are outlined in Table 17. These rates may be exceeded in the case of assets used in multiple shift operations.

Current provisions for accelerated rates of depreciation were originally instituted in 1951. They were superseded in 1957 by a special deduction wherein 10 percent of the excess of new capital investment over the year's depreciation could be taken. The deduction was in addition to regular depreciation and could not exceed 5 percent of income. It remained in effect through the end of 1959 when it was replaced by the original system of acceleration, which is that in effect at present. The accelerated allowances apply to the cost of assets acquired after January 1, 1946, and to investment for the expansion, conversion, and reconstruction of assets acquired either before or after that date. The normal period of depreciation may not be reduced by more than 40 percent. For a period of four years, starting with the first year of an asset's useful life, an additional amount, not to exceed 15 percent of the asset's cost, is added to the regular depreciation deduction in each year.

Depreciation allowances are granted for income tax purposes only if depreciation is recorded in the books of account and in a plant register. Provided that the asset has not been fully depreciated, deductions can be taken as long as the asset remains in use.

Belgium

The tax laws in Belgium are liberal in their treatment of depreciation for tax purposes. Rates of depreciation, applied almost exclusively by the straight-line method, have been kept flexible, and incentive allowances are provided which make it possible to deduct more than 100 percent of the cost of assets. The wartime and immediate postwar rise in prices led to an asset revaluation in 1947 on all assets acquired prior to 1941, and subsequent deductions for depreciation are made on the basis of this revaluation. Accelerated rates of depreciation can be applied only in the case of maritime and inland vessels at a rate of 20 percent in the first year, 15 percent in each of the next two years and 10 percent in each of the next eight years. Allowable depreciation is limited to the amount shown on the books.

Rates of depreciation are negotiated between the revenue authority and individual taxpayers, so that the conditions under which an asset is employed in an individual enterprise are taken into account in determining its useful life. Representative depreciation rates are in the range of from 10 to 20 percent on industrial machinery and equipment, 3 to 5 percent on industrial buildings and 20 to 25 percent on cars and trucks. The length of life for most machinery and equipment varies from seven to ten years.

The incentive allowance provided under the Belgian tax law consists of 30 percent of the amount by which a new productive investment during the year exceeds the sum of: (1) the year's depreciation on property in use at the end of the previous tax year and, (2) the amount obtained from the sale of land, buildings, machinery, etc., sold during the year. The allowance is spread over three years at 10 percent per year and unused portions may be carried foward over a period of five years. The allowance is in addition to normal depreciation so that assets may be depreciated at 130 percent of cost. Only industrial firms engaged in direct production qualify for the allowance. Further, since the incentive has as its objective the expansion of industry, investment in machinery and equipment for replacement purposes does not qualify. During the first year of their operation, new firms may apply the allowance to the entire amount of productive investment made.

Japan

During the immediate post-World War II period, Japan experienced a wild inflation. This began to a lesser extent during the war as prices were more than doubled between 1940 and 1945. However, within one year after the end of the war prices had quadrupled; in the next year, 1947, they again tripled. This fantastic skyrocketing process continued until 1951 when prices were more than 342 times as high as they were in 1935.[8] As a consequence, the book value of assets acquired before the war was virtually meaningless.

The following table indicates the degree of Japanese inflation in the war and postwar periods.

TABLE 18

TOKYO WHOLESALE PRICE INDEX (1934–1936 = 100)

Year	Price Index	Year	Price Index
1935	99.4	1948	12,792.6
1940	164.1	1949	20,876.4
1945	350.3	1950	24.680.7
1946	1,627.1	1951	34,253.1
1947	4,815.2	1956	35,796.7

Source: Statistics Bureau, Bank of Japan.

The need for asset revaluation was recognized by economists and businessmen as early as 1947 and definite proposals were first drawn up in 1948 and 1949. The Allied Powers sent a group of American economists, headed by Professor Shoup of Columbia University, to Japan to study the problem and to make recommendations for its solution. The resulting recommendations included a major suggestion of compulsory revaluation with a 6 percent tax attached to subsequent write-ups.

In 1950 the Diet passed the first in a series of revaluation laws. The objectives were: (1) to adjust conspicuous differences between the book value and the actual value of fixed assets resulting from inflationary trends after the war; (2) to establish a fair distribution in the burden of taxation; (3) to provide a firm structure of corporate capital through the legal enforcement of adequate depreciation as provided by law; (4) to correct undue disparity between old and new stockholders.[9] The revaluation was carried out by applying a determined multiple to the acquisition cost of the asset.

The 1950 law incorporated the Shoup recommendation with the exception that revaluation was made voluntary. The 6 percent tax was to be paid in a three-year span for corporations and a five-year period for individuals. The gain from revaluation was to be set aside in a special reserve account on the company balance sheet for a five-year period. Seventy-five percent of the gain could be used after two years. Assets were allowed to be revalued individually, thus allowing for variation in the value taken. A number of price indices were used for computation on various assets.

The law was not well received and only 32,271 of the 166,122 firms revalued. In 1951, an amendment to the law was passed wherein the effective date for revaluation was changed to that year, but not too many firms revalued. The reasons given were: (1) poor business conditions, and (2) the size of the revaluation tax. With the further increase in prices in 1953, another amendment was introduced to adjust for the increase and liberalization was introduced in regard to capitalization of the gains and payment of the tax. Business firms, however, remained somewhat apathetic to these efforts.

In 1954, the Government made revaluation compulsory for larger corporations (50 million yen capital investment) and reduced the revaluation tax to 3 per cent on a portion of the revaluation write-up. This facilitated the replacement of corporate assets by requiring corporations to charge sufficient depreciation in their records. The provisions of the 1954 law proved to be effective. Small businesses which were not covered were allowed to facilitate revaluation of their assets with the passage of comparable legislation directed toward them in 1957.

Japan also passed laws in 1952 dealing with the modernization of industry. The general objective was not only the modernization of machinery and equipment, but also reduction of the unit input of raw materials and fuels, as well as improvement of product quality and increase of labor productivity.

The following two articles taken from the law indicate how the objectives were to be achieved.

1. Article 6, *Law for Promotion of Rationalization of Enterprise*
Those basic industries designated by government decree as being in urgent need of modernization are permitted in accordance with the Special Taxation Measures Law to apply special depreciation to machinery and equipment purchased and/or manufactured for the purpose of modernizing and expanding operations.

2. Article 43, *Special Taxation Measures Law*
. . . the limit of depreciation for the rationalization of machines, etc., is to be computed according to the provisions and ordinances of the Corporation Tax Law, for an accountable period (from the day such machines have been put into service), and shall be, notwithstanding these provisions, the amount equivalent to one half of the acquisition cost for modernizing the said machines, . . .

Japanese depreciation laws provide for three write-off procedures, the straight-line method, the declining-balance method and the production method. The last method applies only to fixed assets used in the mining industry. Rates of depreciation or the useful lives of assets are set by government authority and must be adhered to unless specific permission for the use of shorter lives is granted. Some typical useful lives and rates of depreciation under the declining-balance system are outlined in the table on p. 70.

The Japanese tax law makes provision for accelerated depreciation at a rate of $33\frac{1}{3}$ percent during the first year on certain types of equipment for the basic heavy industries, the research industries and agriculture. The effect of this first year allowance, which is in addition to regular depreciation, is to shorten the overall period of depreciation. Regular depreciation and this first-year allowance, together, must not be in excess of one-half of the corporation's pre-depreciation taxable income. No incentive allowances are provided by the tax law.

Netherlands

In the Netherlands specific rates of depreciation have not been set down but are determined through negotiation between the taxpayer and the revenue authority. Technological obsolescence is accounted for in useful-life determination and the asset's original cost is used as the basis for depreciation. Conventional rates of depreciation include machinery and equipment, laboratory equipment and furniture, all at 10 percent, and buildings at $1-1\frac{1}{2}$ to 3 percent. Both the straight-line and reducing-balance methods of depreciation are permissible, but once a specific method is chosen it must be adhered to over the life of the asset.

The tax law in the Netherlands allows accelerated depreciation, used at the taxpayer's discretion. Up to 33⅓ percent of the cost of an asset acquired, improved, ordered or contracted for after December 31, 1949, may be written off on an accelerated basis. Under a formula adopted in January 1960, the accelerated rates are applied to machinery and equipment over the first four years at 8⅓ percent per year. The rate for buildings, automobiles and office equipment was set at 6 percent for the first five and one-half years, with 3⅓ percent allowed in the sixth year. Total

TABLE 19

JAPAN: TYPICAL USEFUL LIVES AND DECLINING-BALANCE RATES
OF DEPRECIATION

Type of Machinery and Equipment	Estimated Life in Years	Declining-Balance Rates of Depreciation
Iron and Steel Industry:		
Blast Furnace	17	12.7%
Open Hearth Furnace	18	12.0
Electric Furnace	12–16	17.5–13.4
Metal Products Industry:		
Boring and Turning Mills	12–17	17.5–12.7
Radial Drills	12	17.5
Wire Drawing Machines	12–13	17.5–16.2
Textile Industry:		
Carding Machines	11–13	18.9–16.2
Combers	13	16.2
Looms	13–15	16.2–14.2
Knitting Machines	13–17	16.2–12.7

Source: *Treasury Memorandum on Foreign Depreciation Systems*, p. 711.

depreciation, normal and accelerated, may not exceed the asset's total cost. When accelerated depreciation is applied, the remaining two-thirds of the asset's cost are depreciated on a normal basis. Once the accelerated rate is claimed it must be continued. It is interesting that depreciation at accelerated rates may begin at the date the asset is contracted for, whereas in other countries they begin with the use of the asset.

A special investment incentive is provided under the tax law, whereby a percentage of new investment is deducted from taxable profits. The allowance has no connection with depreciation and only business assets or capital investments qualify. For assets ordered after April 29, 1960, the allowance is 5 percent of cost for each of the first two years. As a result, 110 percent of an asset's cost can be recovered.

Sweden

Fiscal policy is now used extensively in Sweden to encourage investment and to counteract business cycles. Depreciation-tax policies, even with a number of restrictions introduced after 1951, grant the business community more freedom than in other nations.[10]

From 1938 to 1951, the Swedish Government allowed companies or taxpayers to write off the cost of their assets at their own discretion. It was the opinion that friction between the two parties involved, the Government and businessmen, would thus be avoided. However, the policy was regarded as a possible contributor to the country's inflationary problems and the Royal Commission decided that unrestricted depreciation would have to be curtailed. The first restrictive measure was introduced in 1951 as a temporary policy. A 10 percent penalty was imposed on depreciation taken in excess of 10 percent of expenditures on machinery and equipment. From 1952 to 1954 the write-off was allowed at 20 percent on a straight-line basis.

In 1955 the first permanent system of depreciation was inaugurated in Sweden. Under the system, two methods of computing depreciation are allowed: "book depreciation," which is a modified version of the declining-balance method, and "planned depreciation," which is the familiar straight-line method applied to the estimated life of an asset. Under the book depreciation method, plant and equipment can be depreciated at any rate chosen by the taxpayer subject to a maximum limitation of 30 percent of the book value of the asset. A second limitation indicates that the annual write-off should not be less than 20 percent of original cost. Therefore, the cost of machinery and equipment must be written off completely in five years. A special concession is allowed in the case of short-lived assets (those with an estimated life of three years or less) wherein their entire cost may be written off upon acquisition. Rates applied to buildings are individually negotiated but the characteristic rate is from 1½ to 3 percent, applied on a mandatory straight-line basis. No acceleration is granted in addition to that provided by the book depreciation system, and no provision is made for adjustment to price-level changes.

Under the Swedish tax law taxpayers may recover more than 100 percent of the cost of an asset. This is made possible through an incentive-

F

type provision in the tax law, wherein business firms are allowed to set aside up to 40 percent of pre-tax income as an "investment reserve for economic stabilization." The reserve is controlled by the Labor Market Board and its use is determined by prevailing economic conditions. Funds allocated to the reserve are deductible for tax purposes. A firm using the reserve with the Board's permission is granted a special investment allowance of 10 percent of the amount of the reserve used. Amounts so drawn from the reserve are not restored to the firm's taxable income. Thus, the aggregate tax-free allowance on investments financed from the reserve is 110 percent of cost.

Norway

The only method of depreciation allowed in Norway is the straight-line method. It is applied in an unusual manner for in order to claim depreciation the write-off must be entered in the commercial account or drawn from a depreciation reserve specially set up. The funds set aside for capital investment during the three subsequent years make up this reserve. Fifteen percent of the amount drawn from this fund is exempt from taxation. Unused allowances may be carried forward. Rates of depreciation are prescribed by the revenue authorities. They are fixed for the various classes of assets on the assumption that these assets will be maintained in a reasonable state of repair.

The tax law provides for an initial allowance to be applied to buildings and plants, machinery and equipment to be used for the production of goods or the construction and repair of aircraft or ships. The maximum limit on the allowance is 25 percent of the asset's total cost, less a deduction of 500,000 kroner. The initial depreciation can be claimed from the year in which the building work starts, up to and including the fifth year of the plant's operation. Initial depreciation in any one year cannot be in excess of 50 percent of the firm's taxable profits.

The tax law also provides for additional depreciation on all assets which qualify for normal depreciation, with the exception of certain specified assets such as automobiles, trucks, office buildings, and hotels. The additional allowances are claimed in the first five years of an asset's use and are limited to 50 percent of ordinary depreciation and to 2 percent of the asset's total cost. If initial depreciation is claimed, additional allowances may not be claimed.

Denmark

The taxpayer in this country is allowed a good deal of freedom in deducting depreciation costs. The method used on most assets, such as machinery, equipment, fixtures, vehicles, and ships, is the declining-balance method. The amount of write-off for assets treated with this method is left to the taxpayer's option with the stipulation that a maximum of 30 percent of the value of the asset may be claimed in any one year.

In regard to buildings, a 40 percent deduction of acquisition cost may be written off at the taxpayer's discretion over a ten-year period as long as the limit of 10 percent for any one year is observed. A 30 percent deduction of the contract price may be claimed. Here, again, a ceiling of not more than 15 percent is allowed in any one year. An initial allowance is granted on industrial plants and buildings if the investment exceeds 1,000,000 kroner. Thirty percent of the cost over the minimum may be depreciated at a maximum rate of 15 percent in any one year. On new purchases of assets to be used in production (buildings excluded) depreciation at a 50 percent rate may be claimed over the first five years, limited to a maximum of $33\frac{1}{3}$ percent in any one year.

Finland

The straight-line and declining-balance methods are used in this country. If the asset was acquired before January 1, 1956, the straight-line method is applied at a negotiated rate. If, on the other hand, the asset was acquired after January 1, 1956, the declining-balance method is applied within the range of from 12 percent to 30 percent of historical cost. Buildings which do not qualify under the latter stipulation are allowed the following write-offs: wooden, $2\frac{1}{2}$ percent; brick, $1\frac{1}{2}$ percent. Factories, plants, etc., may claim a higher rate: wooden, $5\frac{1}{2}$ percent and brick $2\frac{1}{2}$ percent. If the factory was built in 1958 or later, 30 percent is allowed to be deducted over a four-year period. The 70 percent which remains may be claimed under the straight-line method. If an asset has the estimated life of three years or less, the entire amount may be written off in the year of acquisition. Ships constructed in Finland may be depreciated at the rate of 120 per cent of cost whereas those imported are depreciated at a 60 percent rate. Freedom of limitation is allowed for new machinery purchased from 1958 to 1967, if it is to be utilized in the northern areas of Finland. Requests for additional allowances may be granted if a satisfactory cause is presented to the tax authorities.

Luxembourg

In Luxembourg revaluation coefficients were prescribed in 1959 and depreciation was adjusted on the following basis:

Acquisition Date	Coefficient
1944–1946	1.5
1947–1948	1.3
1949–1950	1.2
1951–1956	1.1

New investment undertaken in 1959 and 1960 may qualify for a write-off of 20 percent of cost. This deduction, however, must not exceed five million francs in any two consecutive years and must be spread over a four-year period.

Normal rates of depreciation are not rigidly specified and both the straight-line and declining-balance method are allowed.

Switzerland

No revaluation provision is granted in Switzerland owing to a change in currency values. Initial and investment allowances are also absent in the tax laws.

Both the straight-line and declining-balance method may be used in making deductions. Rates, although negotiable, are customarily agreed upon as follows: commercial buildings, 2 percent; industrial buildings, 5 percent; plant and machinery, 20 percent; special machinery subject to excessive wear and tear, 30 percent: loose tools, 35 percent. If the straight-line method is used these rates are reduced by one-half.

Austria

In Austria a revaluation of all assets was permitted in 1954 at the then current values. The straight-line method for computing depreciation is most prevalent for assets with a life of less than ten years. In some cases, however, the declining balance method is permissible. Rates of depreciation are negotiable and are agreed to individually by the taxpayer and the Internal Revenue Service. Nevertheless, customary rates are assigned to groups of assets of the same general nature. Obsolescence is taken into consideration when the rates are negotiated. Further, if an asset is used in a number of shifts additional deductions ranging from 20 to 50 percent are allowable.

Austria, too, has introduced the idea of the initial allowance into the tax system. Rates of 20 to 50 percent on fixed assets and 40 to 60 percent on movable assets are allowed. This concession applies to investment undertaken during the period 1957 to 1963.

Australia

The two most common methods of computing depreciation, viz., the declining-balance and the straight-line methods, are used in Australia. The taxpayer is allowed to elect between the two systems, but in the event that no specific preference is voiced, the declining-balance method is required. Methods may be changed at any time.

In 1957, a liberalization of rates under the declining-balance system was put into effect. Rates of depreciation at 150 percent of the straight-line rates are applicable for the depreciation of an asset when the declining-balance method is used.

Rates of depreciation on machinery and plant are determined by the Commissioner of Taxation and are based on his estimate of useful life under normal usage without recognition of obsolescence. A schedule of rates is published for average categories of assets used under average conditions on the basis of a normal workday. These rates are adopted unless the taxpayer petitions for individual consideration. If assets are used in multiple-shift operations, additional depreciation is allowed. In general, rates of depreciation fixed by the Commissioner are found to be somewhat lower than those necessary to provide for capital costs in actual practice.[11] Examples of standard straight-line depreciation rates are commercial aircraft at 25 percent, automobiles and trucks 15 percent, and industrial machinery 5 percent.

The tax law provides for a number of special rates of depreciation. A statutory rate of 33⅓ percent is allowed for plant and machinery used exclusively for scientific research. Investment by firms in facilities exclusively for employees' use also receives a 33⅓ percent rate. These rates are increased to as much as 50 percent when the declining-balance method is used. Plant and buildings used in primary production (i.e., land cultivation, livestock maintenance, fishing operations, etc.) may be written off in five years or at a 20 percent straight-line rate. Plant and equipment used in mining operations can, at the taxpayer's option, be written off in one year, or amortized over the life of the mine.

As a result of a 20 percent investment allowance granted under the Australian tax law, it is possible to deduct 120 percent of the cost of the manufacturing plant for tax purposes. The incentive allowance is intended to encourage productive investment and applies to new manufacturing machinery and equipment acquired after February 7, 1962. Buildings and structural improvements do not qualify for the allowance.

New Zealand

In New Zealand depreciation is allowed on fixed assets and may be taken according to any one of four methods: the declining-balance, straight-line, the sinking-fund method or the renewal-reserves method. The sinking-fund method is not used extensively but is particularly applicable to public utilities. Under the renewal-reserves approach sums are set aside as a general provision toward meeting the cost of future renewals. Buildings are depreciated on a straight-line basis, while most other major assets use the declining-balance method. Rates of depreciation are set by the Commissioner of Taxation. Examples of representative rates are machinery and plant 10 percent, and furniture and fixtures 7½ percent.

New Zealand first introduced special allowances in 1945 in addition to normal depreciation. An allowance of 30 percent is provided and its spread varies with the cost of the asset. For example, if an asset costs up to £300, the 30 percent allowance may be taken in the first year; in the case of an asset costing between £601 and £1,000, the allowance must be spread over three years at 10 percent each year. An initial allowance of 30 percent is granted on all farming assets.

Ceylon

A rather inflexible rate system is found in this country. Most rates of depreciation are listed on a schedule published by the Government and only in the event of an unlisted asset are rates negotiable. Accelerated depreciation is found in certain lump-sum allowances which are provided, e.g., cars at 80 percent. A "development rebate," in some cases 40 percent of investment costs, is allocated to assets which contribute to the development of business within Ceylon.

India

The Income Tax Act in India allows normal depreciation on all types of assets. Depreciation rates are set by the Central Board of Revenue and vary with the type of asset and the conditions of its use. The conventional rate on most types of machinery is 10 percent based on the declining-balance method, which is the only system of depreciation in use at present. Allowable write-off rates for different categories of plant and machinery are as follows:

General plant and machinery	7%
Machinery used in textile industries, paper mills, electrical engineering work, iron and steel industries, cement works, electric supply undertakings, etc.	10
Machinery used in factories for the manufacture of rubber and plastics	12

Process plants for mineral oil refineries   12%
Surface and underground machinery in mines and
    quarries   15

The firm's depreciation allowance, based on the original cost of an asset, is calculated by using a percentage of the above rates, depending on the extent to which the asset was used during the year. If it was in operation for 180 or more days the above rates are applied at 100 percent; from 30 to 180 days at 50 percent and nil for 30 or less days. Seasonal industries are allowed the full annual rate even though they may have operated for less than 180 days. Extra allowances are granted for assets used in multiple-shift operations.

As a means of stimulating private investment, the Government of India has initiated a number of tax concessions. Chief among them is a five-year tax holiday on profits from new industrial undertakings, the amount of exempt profits in any one year being limited to 6 percent of the capital employed in the new business. Dividends paid from such profits are also tax-exempt in the hands of shareholders.

As in the case of Ceylon, "development rebates" have been introduced in India. They are granted on all new plant and machinery and are in addition to normal and extra-shift depreciation allowances but do not reduce the value of the asset for depreciation purposes. Plant and machinery installed before April 1, 1961 receives a rebate of 25 percent of original cost, whereas a 20 percent rebate applies to plant and machinery installed after March 31, 1961. To insure that the rebate will have its intended effect of stimulating productive investment, an amount equal to 75 percent of all such allowances must be placed in a reserve fund to be used during a minimum period of eight years for the sole purpose of productive business investment. As a result of the rebate provision, it is possible to recover 125 percent of an asset's cost.

Inability to utilize full depreciation due to low profits or business loss is accounted for by a provision that allows the deficiency to be carried forward indefinitely.

Pakistan

Pakistan makes provision for liberal depreciation allowances, particularly in the early years of an asset's useful life. Depreciation, based on original cost, is computed according to the declining-balance system. Investment in plant and machinery not previously used in Pakistan receives an initial allowance of 25 percent which is taken in addition to regular depreciation. Plant and machinery installed between April 1,

1948 and June 30, 1961 can be depreciated at double the normal rates during the first five years of the asset's useful life. Commercial and industrial buildings, other than residential structures for industrial employees, constructed between April 1, 1946 and June 30, 1961, receive a 15 percent initial allowance while provision is made for a 25 percent allowance on residential construction for industrial personnel, built between April 1, 1954 and June 30, 1961. Machinery and equipment used in multiple-shift operations is accorded extra allowances. Depreciation at 50 percent above the regular rate is granted on assets used in double-shift work and at 100 percent for triple-shift operations. Where allowable depreciation cannot be used due to insufficient earnings or business losses, the unused portion may be carried forward indefinitely.

African Nations

At this time the African nations are experimenting with various tax policies in order to determine the most efficient and suitable systems both in the long and short run. Most of their methods already adopted have been derived from observation of the tax procedures in more developed nations with much consideration given to their own economic situation. The loss of revenue resulting from the application of concessions or exemptions is a major consideration. The alternative between increased government revenue through taxation or increased development and expansion through exemption is being weighed in deciding what policy is most feasible for the economic well-being of the country.[12]

In Nigeria amounts charged by a firm in its accounts for the depreciation of its capital equipment cannot be deducted from profits for tax purposes. Instead, capital allowances are granted at rates which are established by law or through negotiation between the taxpayer and the Inland Revenue authorities. Initial, annual and balancing allowances provide for the asset's cost over its useful life. Annual allowances are figured on a reducing or declining-balance basis.

The declining-balance and straight-line systems of depreciation are most commonly used in the African nations. Southwest Africa and Ghana, for example, apply the declining-balance method, whereas South Africa applies either of the two methods at the option of the taxpayer.

The practice of granting subsidies to new industries through whole or partial exemptions from the income tax has become popular in many underdeveloped nations. This idea was adopted in both Nigeria and Ghana in 1952. Ghana provides a system of accelerated depreciation under the form of initial allowances, 40 percent allowed on manufacturing plant, 20 percent on mining equipment, and 10 percent on buildings. This initial allowance is in addition to the normal annual allowance which is 10 percent on buildings and which on other assets is figured according to their estimated life. A minimum of 15 percent is stipulated for mining expenditures.

In the tax provisions of Ghana and Nigeria a "holiday" period is provided, during which a company or taxpayer receives tax relief or exemption. In Ghana the holiday period runs for five years, the first five years of a company's existence, whereas Nigeria has initiated a holiday period of two years' duration.

Latin American Nations

The nations of Latin America are, in most cases, in a more advanced stage of economic development than prevails in Africa, Here, too, are found the needs for development and expansion.

There is great interest in Latin America in the use of depreciation deductions as a method of stimulating investment and tax incentives are becoming increasingly popular. Asset-revaluation provisions are common as most Latin American countries have experienced a considerable degree of inflation since World War II. Chile's prices in 1954 were six times those of 1946 while Argentina and Brazil saw a quadruple increase in prices during the period and Colombia and Mexico experienced a doubling of prices.

Argentina

In Argentina the straight-line method of depreciation is used exclusively at rates stipulated by the Government. Where justification exists, rates are negotiable. Special depreciation allowances are granted on tangible fixed assets used in the steel and petrochemical industries. Sixty-six and two-thirds percent of their value may be taken in the first half of their estimated life.

A law for the revaluation of assets was enacted on February 15, 1960. Revaluation coefficients are specified as a maximum and the taxpayer can use a lower coefficient if he so desires. Future depreciation on revalued assets must be figured on the new values in relation to their remaining useful life. The established system of coefficients is as follows:

Financial year of purchase, construction or production	*Maximum Revaluation Allowed*
1944 and earlier	30.0 times
1945	25.0 times
1946	21.0 times

Financial year of purchase, construction or production	Maximum Revaluation Allowed
1947	18.0 times
1948	16.0 times
1949	12.0 times
1950	9.2 times
1951	6.6 times
1952	4.7 times
1953	4.5 times
1954	4.3 times
1955	3.8 times
1956	3.4 times
1957	2.7 times
1958	2.0 times
1959	1.0 times

Prior to 1960 revaluation of the annual depreciation allowance rather than the asset was customary in Argentina.[13] In addition to normal depreciation figured on the basis of estimated useful life, extraordinary allowances were permitted as a percentage of the normal write-off to account for the increased costs of replacement. Assets acquired in 1944 or earlier, for example, received normal depreciation plus an additional amount equal to 500 percent of the normal. The additional allowance for assets acquired in 1947 was 300 percent of normal depreciation. The rates were then graduated downward to a low of 30 percent of assets acquired in 1958.

Brazil

In Brazil, depreciation allowances are limited to movable property. The straight-line method of computing write-offs is the most commonly used, although it is not the only method permissible. Rates of depreciation are not specified for many types of property, but some customary rates are as follows:[14]

Office furniture and machinery	10%
Industrial and agricultural material, equipment and tools	10
Automobiles and other vehicles	20
Electrical installations	20
Ships	5

Rates on machinery and equipment may be increased by 50 percent if such assets are employed for two eight-hour shifts per day. Rates are doubled on assets used for three eight-hour shifts daily. If an asset must be retired owing to unserviceableness or obsolescence, its net book value may be deducted from gross revenues in arriving at taxable income.

According to the tax regulations issued in 1959, the National Institute of Technology establishes criteria for determining the useful life of capital equipment in a given industry. Further, the Executive is given the authority to fix accelerated depreciation rates to be applied to particular sectors of economic activity or to specific industries, for the purpose of stimulating re-equipment and modernization.[15]

Book values of capital assets may be adjusted to account for price-level changes within the limits of official tables approved by the National Economic Council every two years. The basis of the adjustment is cost, and depreciation must be accounted for. Should an unused balance result from the adjustment under the specified coefficients, it must be capitalized and is subject to a 10 percent tax. This tax is not an allowable charge for ordinary income tax purposes.

Chile

The straight-line method of depreciation is used in this country and rates of depreciation under broad categories have been fixed by the tax authorities. Machinery is written off at 5 percent, tools and instruments at 15 to 30 percent, automobiles at 10 percent and organization expenses at 20 percent. Rates are open to negotiation between the taxpayer and the tax authorities and where necessary, exceptional rates or special write-off methods are allowed.

The tax law makes provision for an annual revaluation of the total capital employed in certain businesses. The revaluation is in local currency and is based on the variation between the official cost of living index in the calendar month immediately preceding the balance sheet date and that in the same month of the previous year. No incentive allowances or acceler-ated depreciation are provided.

Colombia

In Colombia, depreciation deductions are computed on a fixed and constant percentage of cost which customarily is 5 percent annually on buildings, 10 percent on machinery and equipment and 20 percent on rolling stock. On particular types of assets, rates may vary from these norms where justified. Assets not producing income are not to be de-preciated. Assets may be written off only to the extent of 90 percent of cost. The remaining 10 percent is considered salvage value and is to be regained upon disposition.

To provide for the replacement of machinery and equipment acquired prior to June 1, 1957, an income tax deduction is allowed, to exceed neither 15 percent of the previous year's net commercial profits nor 15 percent of the asset's orginal cost.

To stimulate Colombian industrial development, companies established in the basic industries prior to 1965 are granted exemptions up to 100 percent of their basic income tax until 1969. To qualify a company must obtain 60 percent of its raw materials from Colombian sources.

Mexico

Under the Mexican tax law, the original cost or the actual amount of deferred expense is deductible solely on a straight-line basis. Exceptions are made in regard to industries which operate on a multiple-shift basis, e.g., the motion picture industry and industries directly connected with mining operations. To determine allowable depreciation in the mining industry, the cost of the asset used is divided by the total tonnage extracted since the beginning of operations, times the tonnage extracted during the taxable year.

Depreciation rates in Mexico are rigidly set by statute. The annual rate on buildings, construction and permanent improvements made thereto is 5 percent; machinery, equipment, furniture, instruments, scientific apparatus, etc., 10 percent, and vehicles, ships, rolling stock, construction industrial equipment, 20 percent. Changes in these established rates may be made upon appeal to the Treasury Department.

A revaluation of assets was permitted in concurrence with the currency devaluation of April 19, 1954, when a reappraisal of 40 percent of the book value of assets was allowed. The gain in value was to be charged in the revaluation account with a corresponding credit to a surplus account. It was required that advantage of the increased deduction be taken before the end of the first business year ending after October 11, 1954.

Under the Law for Promotion of New or Essential Industries of December 31, 1954, substantial exemptions for various federal taxes were made for enterprises engaged in industrial production considered important to the development of Mexico. Maximum exemption was 40 percent of tax payable.

Other Latin American Nations

Asset revaluation was introduced in both Uruguay and Peru. These two countries have similar depreciation rules in other respects also. Both use the straight-line method exclusively, whereas Venezuela allows both straight-line and declining-balance depreciation. Again, both Uruguay and Peru have regulated rates for application to assets while negotiable rates are provided by Venezuela. No acceleration of depreciation is granted by Uruguay and Peru, but Venezuela provides for an initial allowance. The Venezuelan allowance consists of a credit range of 10 to 25 percent for buildings and equipment of taxpayers who have engaged at least 80 percent of their efforts in specified enterprises. The exact percentage involved is determined by the correspondence of investment to taxable income.

Puerto Rico has experimented widely in its depreciation policy. The tax holiday is in effect, wherein a system of exemptions from income, property, and all municipal tax and licenses provides incentive for new investment in commerce and industry. Puerto Rico has experimented with tax deductions since 1919, but it was not until 1947 that they were put to extensive use. At that time, new industry was granted total exemption until June 30, 1957. Partial exemptions were provided for the succeeding years at rates of 75 percent, 50 percent and 25 percent. After June 30, 1962, these industries were denied exemptions. Established enterprises could qualify if substantial expansion and modernization had been undertaken and if they manufactured certain required products.

EFFECTS OF DIFFERENT DEPRECIATION PRACTICES

From the data presented in Table 11 and from the survey of depreciation practices in many of the industrialized countries of the world, it is apparent that some countries are in a more favorable position than others with respect to depreciation allowances and deductions. Further, prior to the adoption of the new guidelines and investment credit in 1962 by the United States, all of the countries surveyed in Table 11 were at a considerable advantage when compared with the United States. It seems quite certain that these liberal depreciation allowances must be recognized as a contributing factor to the economic growth, investment, and productivity of these countries. This can be demonstrated by a comparison of these macroeconomic variables in the respective countries. However, before this is done there are some preliminary notions which need to be mentioned in order to put the comparison in its proper perspective.

First, and in many ways most important, depreciation practices in themselves do not determine these other macroeconomic variables such as growth and investment. The mere fact that a country has depreciation laws which are most favorable to industrial growth and investment does not necessarily mean that this growth will take place. Other macroeconomic factors such as population, aggregate demand, and the level of income and savings are the major determinants in this respect. However, it is true that given these conditions, favorable depreciation laws will and do facilitate and encourage the rate at which the economy will grow. It is in this manner that depreciation laws and allowances can be considered an

TABLE 20a

CANADA

Year	G.N.P.	Machinery and Equipment	Total Capital Formation	Machinery and Equipment as a percentage of G.N.P.
1950	54	60	48	8.3
1951	63	76	56	9.0
1952	73	84	63	8.6
1953	76	84	70	8.3
1954	75	80	68	8.0
1955	81	80	74	7.4
1956*	91	108	95	8.9
1957	94	116	105	9.2
1958	100	100	100	7.5
1959	105	108	101	7.7
1960	109	112	100	7.7
1961	113	108	99	7.2
1962	122	116	106	7.1

1958 = 100

* From 1956 to 1962 a new series of raw data was used and there were slight differences in the data from 1955 to 1956.

Source: *O.E.E.C. Statistical Bulletin*, January 1961, p. 28; *O.E.C.D. National Accounts, 1955–1962*, Supplement to *General Statistics Bulletin*, March 1964.

important contributing factor to the economic development within a country.

In making such an inter-country comparison it is also important that one does not lose sight of the relative position of the countries. The particular phase or stage of development which is characteristic of a country in a given time period may often be better suited to a faster rate of growth. This becomes more apparent in a comparison of the United States and other industrialized countries, for while the others are developed, they are not as highly developed as the United States. For this reason, a rate of growth in excess of that found in the United States can be expected to exist in many other countries. However, the growth in absolute terms can be expected to run ahead in the highly industrialized country. Difficulties such as these are somewhat reduced by the use of index numbers, but nevertheless these factors cannot be completely eliminated from such a comparison.

TABLE 20b

FRANCE

Year	G.N.P.	Machinery and Equipment	Total Capital Formation	Machinery and Equipment as a percentage of G.N.P.
1950	40	35	33	7.4
1951	50	48	44	8.3
1952	58	53	51	7.7
1953	61	53	55	7.4
1954	64	57	64	7.4
1955	69	65	62	8.0
1956*	77	75	73	8.3
1957	87	89	88	8.8
1958	100	100	100	8.5
1959	110	107	111	8.3
1960	122	120	120	8.4
1961	131	140	136	9.0
1962	145	156	151	9.1

1958 = 100

* From 1956 to 1962 a new series of raw data was used and there were slight differences in the data from 1955 to 1956.

Source: *O.E.E.C. Statistical Bulletin*, January 1961, p. 13; *O.E.C.D. National Accounts, 1955–1962*, Supplement to *General Statistics Bulletin*, March 1964, p. 23.

The postwar conditions in Europe and Japan must also be recognized as having an important effect on the economic trends within those countries since the war. Owing to the destructive force of the war, much of the industrial development in Europe and Japan had to be from the ground up and thus necessitated larger capital outlays than might have otherwise been required. This fact in itself is significant but it takes on added importance because much of the industrial capacity put into use is new and, consequently, efficient. Thus, because of circumstances peculiar to these countries in the postwar period their economic needs and economic development can be expected to differ substantially.

One additional factor which must also be considered is the capital output ratio and how it may differ from country to country. The capital output ratio is a relationship which expresses how much additional capital will be needed to generate one additional unit of output. The

TABLE 20c

GERMANY

Year	G.N.P.	Machinery and Equipment	Total Capital Formation	Machinery and Equipment as a percentage of G.N.P.
1950	41	36	36	9.7
1951	51	47	44	10.2
1952	58	55	51	10.4
1953	62	60	58	10.5
1954	67	67	65	11.1
1955	77	85	81	12.2
1956*	85	91	88	11.7
1957	93	92	92	11.0
1958	100	100	100	11.0
1959	108	110	115	11.3
1960	128	139	140	11.9
1961	140	158	160	12.4
1962	153	174	178	12.5
			1958 = 100	

* From 1956 to 1962 a new series of raw data was used and there were slight differences in the data from 1955 to 1956.

Source: *O.E.E.C. Statistical Bulletin*, January 1961, p. 4; *O.E.C.D. National Accounts, 1955–1962*, Supplement to *General Statistical Bulletin*, March 1964, p. 24.

C.O.R. is often a good indication of the stage of economic development characteristic of a country, and thus it is doubtful that any country has a C.O.R. as low as that of the United States. This fact has obvious implications for growth and investment within the respective countries and must be kept in mind in making the comparisons to be undertaken here.

The actual comparison of trends of a number of macroeconomic variables in countries with differing depreciation provisions will consist of several parts. The first will be a comparison of the growth of G.N.P., spending on machinery and equipment, and equipment as a percentage of G.N.P. for six countries, each of which has differing depreciation practices. These countries include Canada, France, Japan, West Germany, the United Kingdom, and the United States. In order to make legitimate comparison, index numbers have been used with 1958 as the base year.

Tables 20a through 20f contain several noteworthy trends and facts which implicitly tend to support the hypothesis that liberal depreciation

TABLE 20d

GREAT BRITAIN

Year	G.N.P.	Machinery and Equipment	Total Capital Formation	Machinery and Equipment as a percentage of G.N.P.
1950	57	47	48	6.7
1951	63	52	54	6.8
1952	69	52	60	6.3
1953	73	63	68	7.1
1954	78	68	74	7.2
1955	83	73	80	7.2
1956*	90	84	88	7.6
1957	95	94	97	8.2
1958	100	100	100	8.2
1959	104	105	105	8.3
1960	110	110	117	8.2
1961	117	126	131	8.8
1962	122	115	131	7.8

1958 = 100

* From 1956 to 1962 a new series of raw data was used and there were slight differences in the data from 1955 to 1956.

Source: *O.E.E.C. Statistical Bulletin*, January 1961, p. 26; *O.E.C.D. National Accounts, 1955–1962*, Supplement to *General Statistical Bulletin*, March 1964, p. 36.

allowances can be a contributing force for economic growth. In all of the countries studied there was a close relationship between movements in G.N.P., and movements in investment spending. This relationship was positive not only in periods of growth, but also in periods of recession such as those experienced by the United States. Countries such as Germany and France which experienced the most rapid increases in investment spending also had the most substantial increases in G.N.P. An item of significance which showed considerable differences between these countries

G

was the spending on machinery and equipment taken as a percentage of G.N.P. This percentage was by far lowest in the United States (5.1 percent in 1962) when compared with the figures for France and Germany of 10 to 12 percent. In part this difference was due to the differing capital requirements of the individual countries but nevertheless the favorable depreciation policies which characterize these countries were conducive to such growth trends. The degree to which depreciation practices actually

TABLE 20e

UNITED STATES

Year	G.N.P.	Machinery and Equipment	Total Capital Formation	Machinery and Equipment as a percentage of G.N.P.
1950	64	82	68	6.7
1951	74	92	74	6.4
1952	78	92	76	6.1
1953	82	96	80	6.1
1954	81	90	83	5.7
1955	89	100	94	5.8
1956*	94	117	101	6.4
1957	99	123	106	6.4
1958	100	100	100	5.1
1959	108	112	111	5.3
1960	112	119	113	5.4
1961	116	110	113	4.9
1962	124	124	123	5.1
			1958 = 100	

* From 1956 to 1962 a new series of raw data was used and there were slight difference in the data from 1955 to 1956.

Source: *O.E.E.C. Statistical Bulletin*, January 1961, p. 28; *O.E.C.D. National Accounts, 1955–1962*, Supplement to *General Statistical Bulletin*, March 1964, p. 37.

contribute to the growth and investment of a given country is impossible to cite in any precise way. However, the data in Tables 20a–20f considered together with Table 11 seem to indicate that where opportunities for growth present themselves, favorable depreciation practices can be an important factor in the realization of these possibilities. Further, it seems that installations of new capital assets or the replacement of existing facilities with new and more productive assets has been accelerated in countries which provide liberal depreciation laws.

The combination of liberal depreciation practices and other favorable economic factors has fostered a rapid growth and a continued industrialization of many countries in the world, thus allowing them to expand production and to do this efficiently. Table 21, which compares the industrial production indices for these countries, reflects this clearly.

The industrial production indices for the ten countries including the United States which are contained in Table 21 indicate several relevant facts. First, with few exceptions the countries studied were considerably

TABLE 20f

JAPAN

Year	G.N.P.	Machinery and Equipment	Total Capital Formation
1950	40	NA	24
1951	51	NA	36
1952	58	NA	40
1953	68	66	49
1954	74	54	50
1955	82	59	47
1956	90	135	75
1957	101	164	103
1958	100	100	100
1959	120	154	120
1960	141	238	171
1961	172	317	237
1962	190	144	241
		1958 = 100	

Source: *Japanese Economic Statistics*, May-June 1964, p. 47. *Japanese Economic Statistics*, October 1958, p. 27.

Machinery and equipment as a percentage of G.N.P. is not included in this table owing to the differing method of reporting economic statistics; however, the data on machinery and equipment is included because of the importance of the trend of that series.

behind the United States with respect to individual indices in 1950. However, by 1960 the indices of most of the countries had either caught up to or passed the United States. The countries which made the most substantial gains were Germany, Italy, and France. It is interesting to note that these countries are the ones which had the greatest amounts of investment in machinery and equipment relative to their own G.N.P during the latter part of the decade. Table 20b and 20c substantiate this claim for France and Germany and although data on Italy are not included

TABLE 21

INDUSTRIAL PRODUCTION INDEX (1958=100)

Year	France	Belgium	Luxembourg	Netherlands	Germany	Italy	U.K.	U.S.A.	Canada	Sweden
1950	58	82	76	66	47	55	82	80	70	78
1951	66	93	92	69	56	62	87	87	76	82
1952	66	88	91	69	60	84	84	90	79	80
1953	66	87	83	77	65	69	88	99	85	81
1954	73	92	86	87	74	76	94	92	84	85
1955	79	101	96	94	86	83	100	105	93	91
1956	88	108	103	98	92	90	100	108	102	93
1957	96	108	104	100	97	97	101	109	102	98
1958	100	100	100	100	100	100	100	100	100	100
1959	104	104	104	112	111	111	107	114	109	105
1960	115	114	114	127	129	129	114	118	110	112

Source: Robert Theobald, *Business Potential in the European Common Market*, American Management Association (New York), 1963.

TABLE 22

MANUFACTURING IN GENERAL (1953 = 100)

	Year	Employment	Production	Productivity	Wage	Unit Labor Cost
BELGIUM	1955		119	—	106	—
	1957	107	128	120	125	105
	1958	107	120	113	131	112
	1959	100	128	128	131	104
	1960	97	136	139	138	98
	1961	100	145	145	143	99
	1962	102	155	151	154	101
CANADA	1955	97	107	110	107	97
	1957	102	113	111	118	107
	1958	97	111	114	123	107
	1959	98	119	121	127	105
	1960	97	130	134	131	98
	1961	96	134	139	134	96
	1962	100	144	144	138	96
FRANCE	1955	102	118	116	115	99
	1957	106	148	140	134	96
	1958	107	156	146	150	103
	1959	105	158	151	158	105
	1960	105	167	159	169	106
	1961	106	175	165	183	111
	1962	108	192	177	198	122

Table 22—*continued*

	Year	Employment	Production	Productivity	Wage	Unit Labor Cost
WEST	1955	114	130	114	109	96
GERMANY	1957	126	149	118	132	112
	1958	126	154	122	141	115
	1959	127	166	131	145	113
	1960	132	179	136	159	117
	1961	136	190	139	176	125
	1962	137	199	145	196	134
ITALY	1955	105	119	113	110	97
	1957	121	138	114	122	107
	1958	124	143	115	128	111
	1959	130	159	122	131	107
	1960	138	182	132	134	102
	1961	146	202	138	140	101
	1962	150	222	148	155	105
U.K.	1955	105	115	109	111	101
	1957	105	117	111	126	113
	1958	104	116	112	130	116
	1959	105	123	118	140	114
	1960	101	133	131	156	118
	1961	103	133	129	165	127
	1962	102	133	130	172	131
U.S.A.	1955	96	105	109	106	98
	1957	97	109	112	117	104
	1958	90	100	111	120	108
	1959	94	114	121	125	103
	1960	96	119	124	130	104
	1961	93	120	129	134	103
	1962	96	129	134	138	103
JAPAN	1955	109	125	115	108	93
	1957	134	183	137	124	90
	1958	139	184	132	123	94
	1959	155	231	149	134	90

Source: *O.E.E.D. Statistical Bulletin*, March 1964; Raymond L. Staepelaere and R. F. Mikesell, *Common Market Competition in Manufacturing* (Menlo Park, Calif., Stanford Research Center, 1960).

in these tables, it is a fact that in 1959 and 1960, 8.3 percent and 9.5 percent of Italy's G.N.P. was spent on machinery and equipment. The relationship between growth in industrial production and the rate with which new and more efficient capital is put into operation is a highly positive one. It is this relationship which has allowed countries such as Germany and France to make the great strides which they have made during the postwar years. Here again, favorable depreciation laws must be recognized as a contributing factor, for such laws not only tend to encourage the replacement and addition of productive capital, but also allow faster write-offs so that obsolete equipment can be more rapidly replaced.

Another significant measure of the progress of an economy in terms of its adoption and use of newer and more efficient capital is increasing productivity. Table 22, which measures man-hour output, is a good indication of the contribution of modernized plant and equipment to productivity.

To summarize the foregoing material, one finds that depreciation practices differ considerably from country to country and that prior to the tax revisions of 1962 all of the countries studied in Table 11 were in more favorable positions in this respect than the United States. It has been demonstrated that differences in depreciation laws can account for some part of the variation of macroeconomic variables in these countries. Further, depreciation must be recognized as an important contributing factor to the economic climate of any country. This was apparent from developments which followed the Revenue Act of 1962. The Department of Commerce estimated that in 1962 the new guidelines accounted for about $2.4 billion in additional depreciation allowances. Further, total depreciation allowances increased steadily after the tax revision to $27.5 billion in 1962, to $28.8 billion in 1963, and to $30.5 billion in 1964. At the same time, expenditures for new plant and equipment increased from $34.4 billion in 1961 to $37.3 billion in 1962, to $39.2 billion in 1963, and to $44.9 billion in 1964. A logical conclusion is that the increase in depreciation as an important source of investment funds was a significant causal factor of the concurrent expansion of investment and capital formation.

NOTES

[1] Much of the material dealing with foreign systems of depreciation was drawn from the following sources: Statement of Maurice E. Peloubet, "Depreciation Reform," *Tax Revision Compendium*, Compendium of Papers on Broadening the Tax Base, submitted to the Committee on Ways and Means, Committee Print (Washington, 1959), Volume 2, pp. 911–914; Unpublished document prepared by the Minnesota Mining and Manufacturing Company;

John C. Connolly, "Foreign Depreciation Methods," *The Tax Magazine*, March 1960, pp. 175–196; *Depreciation in Foreign Countries*, University of Pennsylvania Tax Conference, September 26, 27, 28, 1961; Memorandum prepared by the Office of Financial Analysis, U.S. Treasury, "Depreciation Practices in Certain Foreign Countries," in *Hearings before the Joint Economic Committee, Congress of the United States*, 87th Congress, 2nd Session, August 17, 1962, pp. 693–719, hereinafter referred to as *Treasury Memorandum on Foreign Depreciation Systems*; Price, Waterhouse & Company, *Information Guide for Those Doing Business in Foreign Countries*. Series of bulletins published between 1960–1963.

[2] Harvey Perry, "Depreciation and Taxes," *Tax Institute*, November 20, 21, 1958.

[3] George Brimmell, "Economy Gets $350 Million Shot in the Arm," *The Telegram*, Toronto, February 5, 1962, p. 16.

[4] Unpublished document prepared by the Minnesota Mining and Manufacturing Company; *Treasury Memorandum on Foreign Depreciation Systems*, p. 702.

[5] Maurice E. Peloubet, "What Would Depreciation Reform Cost?" *The Tax Executive*, October 1960, pp. 41–43.

[6] W. W. Brudno and Frank Bowers, *Taxation in the United Kingdom* (Cambridge, The Riverside Press, 1957).

[7] Robert G. Werthemeimer, "Tax Incentives in Germany," *National Tax Journal*, Vol. 10, December 1957, p. 33.

[8] Sidney Davidson and Yasukichi Yasuba, "Asset Revaluation and Income Taxation in Japan," *National Tax Journal*, Vol. 13, March 1960, pp. 45–58.

[9] 1960 Financial Statement of the Yawata Iron and Steel Company, Ltd., pp. 10–12.

[10] Martin Norr, Frank J. Duffy, Harry Steiner, *Taxation in Sweden*, World Tax Series (Harvard University Law School, 1959).

[11] Walter W. Brudno, *Taxation in Australia*, World Tax Series (Harvard University Law School, 1958); Price, Waterhouse & Company, Bulletin on Australia, pp. 26–28.

[12] See Alan H. Smith, "Tax Relief for New Industry in Ghana," *National Tax Journal*, Vol. 11, 1958, pp. 362–370; Price, Waterhouse & Company, Bulletin on Nigeria, pp. 19–20.

[13] Joseph Froomkin, "Some Problems of Tax Policy in Latin America," *National Tax Journal*, Vol. 11, 1958, p. 370.

[14] Henry J. Gumpel and Rudin Gomez de Sousa, *Taxation in Brazil*, World Tax Series, Harvard University Law School (Cambridge, The Riverside Press, 1957).

[15] Gertrude E. Heare, *Brazil: Information for United States Businessmen*, U.S. Department of Commerce Publication, November 1961, p. 175.

V   *Evaluation of*
Possible Solutions

THERE ARE SEVERAL METHODS of compensating for the deficiency between the level of depreciation accruals and the replacement cost of plant and equipment. Some of these involve changes in the depreciation tax structure, while others provide solutions outside of the area of strict depreciation reform.

SUPPLEMENTS FOR INADEQUATE DEPRECIATION CHARGES

There are several possible expedients to provide for the deficit between the funds supplied by depreciation accruals and the amount needed to replace facilities at current prices. The first is that the necessary funds simply be borrowed. As an emergency measure, this approach may work for a year or two. It must be remembered, however, that the need for capital replacement is an annually recurring problem for many companies. Because of inadequate depreciation allowances, additional funds are needed every year; and no company can go on borrowing large sums year after year, just to stay even, without facing eventual bankruptcy from an inability to meet mounting interest and debt repayment charges. Furthermore, it is highly unlikely that lenders will be willing to continue for any considerable period of time to make additional loans to a company merely for the replacement of existing facilities. There is one set of circumstances, however, where borrowing could be permitted. It would be a valid procedure if the return on the newly installed equipment were exceptionally high; high enough, that is, to pay the interest on the debt and amortize the loan. It is clear, however, that very few facilities are capable of yielding a saving of this magnitude. Hence, few companies are able to secure from prudent lenders on a continuing basis the funds necessary to replace obsolete facilities, and fewer still are able to repay the needed funds if the practice is long continued.

Some words of clarification are in order in connection with the problem of borrowing. It is a fact that many companies do borrow to replace their assets. This is particularly true of those companies which do not have a large, uniform, year-by-year replacement program. There may be a period of three or four years in which no large outlays are made, but in the year following the firm may be confronted with sizable expenditures. Since the depreciation funds accrued over the years may have been used for working capital and may well be no longer available, a loan is often negotiated to finance part or all of the replacement. It is clearly evident, however, that such a loan is not really for the replacement of plant and equipment, but rather a postponed operation which should, strictly speaking, have taken place to provide working capital during the preceding years.

The second expedient, the sale of stock, would at first sight seem to have possibilities, for it has been argued that the actual dollar investment of the original stockholders would be protected since the book value of the company would be increased by the amount of the stock which is sold. For example, if a company were worth a million dollars and issued an additional million dollars in stock to new shareholders in order to obtain necessary capital to replace its old plant, it would appear that the original stockholders still have a million dollars equity in a plant now worth two million. However, the original shareholders, who formerly owned the entire plant, now own only half of it. Further, it cannot be assumed that a much greater volume of goods will be produced since the new facilities are principally a replacement and not an expansion, and earnings will probably remain relatively stable. This means that the amount of dividends paid to the original stockholders will be cut since there are now twice as many shares outstanding over which to spread the same amount of income. Again, as in the case of borrowing, a firm which planned to sell stock to acquire replacement capital will probably experience difficulty in raising the necessary funds. It seems highly unlikely that the prudent investor will readily buy stock in a company which repeatedly has to dilute its equity by the sale of additional shares in order to cover its costs of production. In this connection it must be remembered that wear and tear on facilities is definitely one of the costs of production. Hence, the expedient of selling additional stock to supplement inadequate depreciation accruals seems little, if any, more satisfactory than that of borrowing the necessary funds.

A third expedient, the investment of retained earnings, has in practice provided a partial solution to the difficulty of bridging the gap between depreciation charges and actual replacement costs. This approach, however, has limitations and results in undesirable distortions that are not always fully recognized. If the funds for the necessary replacement of capital assets must be taken from profits, then it is clear that profits have been overstated.

Further, the use of profits for the replacement of productive assets also has an undesirable effect upon prices. Prices must provide enough income for a firm to cover its cost of production, or the company will soon be insolvent. As already stated, wear and tear on capital equipment is a cost of doing business. Unless it is fully provided for, the business is, in effect, subsidizing its customers and actually is in the process of liquidation. As a result, the need to rely on profits to assist in the replacement of equipment constitutes an upward influence on price levels.

METHODS OF DEPRECIATION REFORM

The proposals that were offered for depreciation reform fall into two main categories: those which aimed at offsetting obsolescence through accelerated depreciation based on shorter lives or higher annual write-off rates, and those which offered various means to allow for the declining value of the dollar because of inflation. Ideally, both the length of life and inflation should be taken into account.

SHORTENING USEFUL LIVES

The Defense Production Act of 1940 provided for the issue of certificates of necessity under which the cost of war and defense plants could be written off over a five-year period. This act was not aimed at a solution of the depreciation problem, for, in fact, the problem did not exist at that time. The principal purpose of the act was to allow those who invested in war and defense facilities to recoup their investment in a short time because of the experience of World War I. In the course of that war a number of firms had built plants for military purposes which operated only a short while before the armistice and then had to be shut down or be completely revamped afterwards with considerable loss to the investor.

The rapid amortization policy introduced in 1940 ended with the close of World War II and was not restored until the outbreak of the Korean conflict in 1950. Again it was only applied to those facilities deemed necessary for defense. In 1956 the Government virtually ceased issuing certificates of necessity granting rapid write-offs for defense facilities. This program did make a limited contribution to the solution of the obsolescence aspect of the depreciation problem where facilities that were judged necessary for defense were involved. However, it applied only to these facilities and gradually all of the certificates of necessity granted through 1956 expired.

The act permitting rapid write-offs of defense facilities during World War II and in the Korean situation was primarily an expedient used as an incentive to stimulate investment in plant and equipment needed for the national defense. It was not directed specifically at the question of shorter lives for equipment.

In order to mitigate the difficulties arising from obsolescence, a direct approach to the problem was offered. In 1961 a Bill (S. 580) was introduced by Senator George Smathers and a companion piece of legislation (H.R. 422) was offered in the House of Representatives by Representative Eugene Keogh. These measures attempted to provide a means whereby more realistic economic lives with respect to machinery and equipment would be provided for tax purposes.

Generally known as the Five-Year Write-Off, this proposal offered one of the simplest methods for shortening lives and also provided an incentive to investment expansion. The Bill sought to amend the Internal Revenue Code of 1954 in the following ways:

(1) Taxpayers are allowed to select any period of depreciation they desire, provided this period is not less than five years, for new machinery purchased after December 31, 1960. The minimum period is three years for used equipment (equipment which is two or more years old).

(2) Election of the depreciation period must be made within the time prescribed for filing a return for the year in which the depreciable property is acquired. Although election is irrevocable, it can be selective for each piece of depreciable property.

(3) Salvage value of the property will remain unaffected.

(4) If the property is sold at a price greater than its depreciated book value, any profit larger than that which would result if usual depreciation were charged would be taxed as ordinary income. The balance would be treated as a capital gain.

Perhaps the one difficulty to the Smathers-Keogh proposal was that it required action and approval on the part of the legislature. The useful-lives revision eventually settled upon by the Treasury Department did not require any new legislation and thus went into operation more quickly.

THE USEFUL-LIVES REVISION IN REVENUE PROCEDURE 62-21

In early December 1961, the Treasury Department announced that a survey would be made of some 50 companies in six large and basic industries to determine whether or not changes should be made in Bulletin F (which contained guidelines for the length of life allowed in writing off capital assets). This had actually been started in October of that year when the textile industry was granted some changes:

The six industries investigated were: 1. Aircraft and parts manufacturers, 2. automotive manufacturers, 3. electrical machinery and equipment, 4. metal-working machinery and machine tools, 5. railroads, and 6. the steel industry.

The study constituted an attempt by the Treasury to introduce some flexibility into the length of time during which an asset could be depreciated. Many companies had already taken full advantage of the flexibility as it was provided in Bulletin F, while others for one reason or another had not done so.

The outcome of the study resulted in *Revenue Procedure 62-21* which in July 1962 replaced Bulletin F with a completely new schedule determining the length of useful lives. The new schedule shortened the lives in Bulletin F in some instances by as much as 30 to 40 percent and, as in the case of Bulletin F, it indicated that the new lives were to be considered as guidelines for the depreciation of equipment. In fact, the introduction to *Revenue Procedure 62-21* states:

A central objective of the new Procedure is to facilitate the adoption of depreciable lives even shorter than those set forth in the guidelines, or shorter than those currently in use, provided only that certain standards are met and that subsequent replacement practices are reasonably consistent with the tax lives claimed.

The new Procedure is essentially different from the Bulletin F approach insofar as it applies to broad classifications of plant and equipment rather than individual assets. In general, a length-of-life guideline is set down for a single industry which covers all the production machinery and equipment typically used in that industry. There are about 75 broad classifications of assets, whereas Bulletin F listed guidelines for approximately 5,000 separate items. This broad class approach seeks to achieve "a reasonable overall result in measuring depreciation rather than a needless and labored item-by-item accuracy."[1]

Part I of *Revenue Procedure 62–21* sets forth the guidelines for depreciable property. Depreciable assets are grouped into four broad units which are further divided and subdivided. Group One presents guidelines for assets used by business generally. In its four main divisions, it covers such common business assets as office furniture, fixtures, transportation equipment, land improvements and buildings—except for special-purpose structures that are an integral part of the production process. Group Two covers the assets of non-manufacturing activities, excluding transportation, communications, and public utilities. Its eight major categories encompass agriculture, contract construction, fishing, logging and sawmilling, mining, recreation and amusement, services, wholesale and retail trade. Group Three has thirty major classifications covering activities in manufacturing. It encompasses the whole spectrum of manufacturing from aerospace to vegetable oil products. In Group Four, which consists of twelve major divisions, are found the guidelines for transportation, communications, and public utilities.

The revision affects 70 to 80 percent of business assets which may be depreciated more rapidly than before. It does not disturb the depreciation allowance on 20 to 30 percent of business property on which rates of depreciation have been as rapid, or more rapid, than allowed by the new guidelines. Secretary of the Treasury Dillon estimated that the new lives average 32 percent shorter than those set forth in Bulletin F. A Treasury Department depreciation survey indicated that the new lives are 15 percent shorter than the lives in actual use by 1,100 large corporations at the time of the survey. This is significant because these corporations hold two-thirds of all the depreciable assets in manufacturing. The Treasury Department estimated that many corporations would be able to utilize depreciation write-offs even quicker than those suggested, so that the depreciable lives of their assets would be about 21 percent shorter than those in use in July of 1962.[2]

Under Bulletin F the average depreciable life of manufacturing assets listed was approximately 19 years. However, many companies, through negotiation with the Internal Revenue Service, were able to obtain approval for the use of shorter lives. In July of 1962 it was estimated by the Treasury Department that the actual average life of a manufacturing asset was 15 years. *Revenue Procedure 62–21* shortened this considerably and in its frame of reference the average life of an asset is about twelve years.[3]

A number of industry comparisons can be made of the revised useful lives with those contained in Bulletin F. In the steel industry, for example, the length of life for total productive equipment is now 18 years. Under

Bulletin F, many of the industry's facilities were given a life of 25 years, while some had 20 and, in a few instances, the figure ran as high as 30. In printing, the new lives are 11 years whereas formerly a number of assets, particularly presses, were depreciated over a twenty- to twenty-five year period. There were, however, a number of items that had substantially shorter lives which even fell beneath the new eleven-year guideline. In chemical and allied products the new guideline is 11 years. In comparing this with Bulletin F, there is a substantial reduction for many assets. However, as in the printing industry, there were also a large number of items with lives below the current eleven-year standard. A comparison of Bulletin F with the new regulation indicates that significant reductions in useful life have, for the most part, been given to heavy equipment.

The object of the revision and the philosophy of the Administration is summed up in the introduction to *Revenue Procedure 62–21*:

The administrative revision of depreciation guidelines and practices contained in this Procedure is based on a recognition that depreciation reform is not something which can be accomplished once and for all time. It reflects an administrative policy dedicated to a continuing review and up-dating of depreciation standards and procedures to keep abreast of changing conditions and circumstances.

Initially a three-year period free of supervision from the Internal Revenue Service was provided for taxpayers to adapt their practices to the new guidelines. After this period of grace, taxpayers were to meet a "reserve-ratio" test if they used a life lower than that stipulated in the guidelines. The Treasury Department devised the reserve-ratio test to determine the consistency or inconsistency of the taxpayer's retirement and replacement procedures relative to the length of life claimed. It intended to assure that his replacement practices corresponded with the actual useful life of his depreciable assets. However, both the moratorium period and the reserve-ratio test were viewed with a good deal of apprehension and were widely criticized by the business community. Generally, it was felt that the three-year moratorium period was too short, and it was noted that the reserve-ratio test contained technical defects, the principal one being the assumption of an even rate of growth each year. The reserve ratio was also considered to be much too complex. In 1965, in order to rectify this situation, the Treasury introduced a number of modifications to the 1962 plan which are currently in force.

THE RESERVE-RATIO TEST

Basically, the reserve-ratio test is an arithmetical formula or ratio of the accumulated depreciation reserves for the assets in any guideline class to the basis or original cost of those assets. Taking into account the depreciation method employed, the service life of the assets, and the growth rate of the gross stock of depreciable facilities,[4] the value of this "calculated" reserve ratio is considered against the "appropriate" reserve-ratio range as given in a special reserve-ratio table. If the firm's ratio exceeds the upper limit of the appropriate range, it is concluded that the retirement and replacement of its assets is not consistent with the class life used.

As an illustration of the reserve-ratio test, assume a hypothetical business situation in which a shipbuilding firm is applying the test. The firm is depreciating its capital equipment purchased at an original cost of $3,000,000 and thus far has accumulated $1,500,000 in depreciation reserves using the straight-line method of depreciation. It applies the reserve-ratio test to determine whether or not its retirement practice is consistent with the class life used.

As was noted, the first major component of the test, the reserve ratio, is the ratio of the depreciation reserves for the assets in the guideline class to the basis or original cost of those assets. In the case of the shipbuilding firm, its accumulated reserves of $1,500,000 are divided by $3,000,000, the original cost of its assets, giving a reserve ratio of $\frac{1}{2}$ or 50 percent.

$$\text{Reserve Ratio} = \frac{\text{Total depreciation reserves for all assets in class}}{\text{Total basis of all assets in class}}$$

$$\text{Reserve Ratio} = \frac{1,500,000}{3,000,000} = \tfrac{1}{2} \text{ or } 50\%$$

The firm must next determine the appropriate reserve-ratio range. To do this it must take into account the method of depreciation being used, the test life of the assets and the rate of growth for the class. The first two of these are easily established but the rate of growth will require some explanation. As has been noted, the straight-line method of depreciation is being used, and according to the suggested guideline as listed in *Revenue Procedure 62–21*, the test life on shipbuilding assets is 12 years. The rate of growth for the class is derived from the Rate of Growth Conversion Table (see Table 23) provided in *Revenue Procedure 62–21*. To use the table it is necessary to determine: (1) the asset ratio for the guideline class; and (2) the class-life period for that class, which has already been established as 12 years. To establish the asset ratio, the total basis or original cost of all the assets in the class during the current taxable year is divided by the total basis of all the assets in the class during the taxable year one class-life period earlier. Let us assume that 12 years, or one class-life period ago, the basis or original cost of the shipbuilding firm's assets was $1,875,000. This figure when divided into $3,000,000, the current basis of its assets, gives an asset ratio of 1.60. Consulting Table 23, the Rate of Growth Conversion Table, the rate of growth is established as 4 percent.

In the next stage of the test, the firm compares its reserve ratio, which

TABLE 23
ILLUSTRATIVE RATE OF GROWTH CONVERSION TABLE

In the appropriate class life period column, find the figure which most closely approximates the asset ratio. The corresponding rate of growth will appear in the marginal columns.

Rates of growth	3	4	5	6	8	10	12	14	16	18	20	Rates of growth
					Class-life period (years)							
Percent												Percent
−4	0.88	0.85	0.82	0.78	0.72	0.66	0.61	0.56	0.52	0.48	0.44	−4
−2	.94	.92	.90	.89	.85	.82	.78	.75	.72	.70	.67	−2
−1	.97	.96	.95	.94	.92	.90	.89	.87	.85	.84	.82	−1
0	1.00	1.00	1.00	1.00	1.00	1.00	1.00	1.00	1.00	1.00	1.00	0
1	1.03	1.04	1.05	1.06	1.08	1.10	1.13	1.15	1.17	1.20	1.22	1
2	1.06	1.08	1.10	1.13	1.17	1.22	1.27	1.32	1.37	1.43	1.49	2
4	1.12	1.17	1.22	1.26	1.37	1.48	1.60	1.73	1.87	2.03	2.19	4
6	1.19	1.26	1.34	1.42	1.59	1.79	2.01	2.26	2.54	2.85	3.21	6
8	1.26	1.36	1.47	1.59	1.85	2.16	2.52	2.94	3.43	4.00	4.66	8
10	1.33	1.46	1.61	1.77	2.14	2.59	3.14	3.80	4.60	5.56	6.73	10

Source: *Depreciation Guidelines and Rules*, p. 36.

it has already established as 50 percent, with the Reserve Ratio Table (Table 24). The factors it must consider are the test life of its assets (12 years), the method of depreciation (straight-line), the rate of growth (4 percent), and the reserve ratio (50 percent). From the table it can be seen that the reserve-ratio range for a class with a twelve-year life and a 4 percent rate of growth is 42–53 percent. Consequently, the shipbuilding firm has met the reserve-ratio test and thus may conclude that its retirement and replacement practice is consistent with the class life used.

In connection with the Reserve Ratio Table (Table 24), it should be

H

noted that the reserve-ratio range permits the taxpayer a degree of latitude in the determination of his depreciable lives. The table shows an appropriate reserve ratio (46 percent in our example) as well as lower and upper limits of 42–53 percent. This margin of tolerance embodied in the table encompasses rates of replacement as much as 20 percent slower than the

TABLE 24

ILLUSTRATIVE RESERVE RATIO TABLE

Section I: Straight-Line Method of Depreciation

Test Life	Rate of growth (percent)										Test Life
	−4	−2	−1	0	1	2	4	6	8	10	
3	51	50	50	50	50	50	49	49	48	48	3
	46–59	45–58	45–58	45–58	45–57	45–57	44–56	44–56	44–55	43–55	
4	51	51	50	50	50	49	49	48	48	48	4
	46–60	46–59	45–59	45–58	45–58	45–57	44–56	44–56	43–55	43–54	
5	52	51	50	50	50	49	48	48	47	46	5
	46–61	46–59	45–59	45–58	45–58	44–57	44–56	43–55	43–54	42–53	
6	52	51	51	50	50	49	48	47	46	45	6
	47–61	46–60	45–59	45–58	45–58	44–57	44–56	43–54	42–53	41–52	
8	53	51	51	50	49	49	47	46	45	44	8
	47–62	46–60	46–59	45–58	45–57	44–57	43–55	42–53	41–52	40–50	
10	53	52	51	50	49	48	47	45	44	42	10
	48–63	46–61	46–59	45–58	44–57	44–56	42–54	41–52	40–50	39–48	
12	54	52	51	50	49	48	46	44	43	41	12
	48–63	47–61	46–60	45–58	44–57	43–56	42–53	40–51	39–48	37–46	
14	55	52	51	50	49	48	46	43	41	39	14
	49–65	47–61	46–60	45–58	44–57	43–55	41–52	40–49	38–47	36–44	
16	55	53	51	50	49	47	45	42	40	38	16
	49–65	47–62	46–60	45–58	44–57	43–55	41–51	39–48	37–45	35–42	
18	56	53	52	50	49	47	44	41	39	36	18
	50–66	47–62	46–60	45–58	44–56	43–54	40–51	38–47	36–43	34–40	
20	57	53	52	50	48	47	44	41	38	35	20
	50–67	48–63	46–61	45–58	44–56	42–54	40–50	37–46	35–42	33–38	

Source: *Depreciation Guidelines and Rules*, p. 37.

tax life used, but only 10 percent faster. The firm's reserve ratio moves toward the upper limit of the appropriate range as the amount of depreciation taken is increased and/or if new investment is not undertaken. In such instances the numerator of the ratio is increased while the denominator remains constant. On the other hand, increased capital investment raises the basis of the assets held, and so lowers the reserve ratio. As the firm's ratio moves below the lower limit of the appropriate range, it is an indication that a shorter useful life on its assets may be justified.

If the firm's reserve ratio exceeds the upper boundary of the appropriate range, it can be subject to a possible revision of its depreciable lives unless it can justify in the light of all the facts and circumstances the maintenance of the claimed lives. This may be done on the basis of previous experience, or prior auditing, or negotiations with the tax authorities. If the claimed lives cannot be so justified, the *Revenue Procedure* permits the firm a period of years equal to its class life to bring its reserve ratio within the appropriate scale, providing that the ratio is moving toward the correct range during this period. The reserve ratio will be judged to be moving in the proper direction if the amount by which it exceeds the appropriate upper limitation is lower than it was for any one of the three preceding taxable years. If the firm does not meet this proviso, its class life may be increased in accordance with an adjustment table provided in the *Revenue Procedure*. The increase can range from one-third for assets with very short lives to one-fourth for most assets. Penalty rates which in the past have been used to correct errors over a brief span of time will no longer be imposed on firms using a faster rate of depreciation than can be justified. Instead the lives will be extended in accordance with the Adjustment Table (see Table 24).

It should be noted that the reserve-ratio test should not be applied rigidly and can, under certain circumstances, be somewhat meaningless. A business might have a reserve ratio above the appropriate level, but this may not be an absolute indication that its practices of retirement and replacement are inconsistent with the class life used. When a taxpayer has relatively few assets in the class, there may be a wide variation in the reserve ratio so that in some years it exceeds the upper limit and in other periods it is beneath the lower boundary. Variations of this nature are possible where there are relatively few assets in the class because some of them may be retired in the same year. Immediately before their removal from service, the ratio would exceed the appropriate upper limitation; after their retirement it would fall beneath the lower level of the range.

As an illustration of this, let us assume the following situation: Company X has only two office machines, each valued at $10,000 with a useful life of 10 years that are depreciated on a straight-line basis. Nine years after the purchase of the machines, $18,000 in depreciation reserves have been accumulated. The reserve ratio, therefore, would be 90 percent $\left(\dfrac{\$18,000}{\$20,000} = \dfrac{9}{10} \right)$. If we assume that the value of the assets ten years earlier (or one class life earlier) was $20,000, then the asset ratio is 1 and the rate of growth is zero. Referring to Table 24 we find that the appropriate reserve-ratio range is 45–58 percent. Consequently our firm has a reserve ratio far in excess of the appropriate upper limitation. In the tenth year, the two machines are replaced by two comparable models also valued at $10,000 apiece. The reserve ratio in that year would be 10 percent $\left(\dfrac{\$\,2,000}{\$20,000} = \dfrac{1}{10} \right)$

Again the rate of growth is zero because the asset ratio is unity, i.e., value same today as 10 years ago. Thus the appropriate range would be still

TABLE 25

ILLUSTRATIVE ADJUSTMENT TABLE FOR CLASS LIVES

Justifying a Shorter Class Life by Low Reserve Ratio		Lengthening the Class Life in Cases where Reserve-Ratio Test is Not Met	
Class Life Used in the Preceding Taxable Year	Appropriate Class Life	Three-year Average Class Life	Appropriate Class Life
3	2.5	3	4
4	3.5	4	5
5	4	5	6.5
6	5	6	7.5
8	7	8	10
10	8.5	10	12.5
12	10	12	15
14	12	14	17.5
16	13.5	16	20
18	15.5	18	22.5
20	17	20	25

Source: *Depreciation Guidelines and Rules*, p. 42.

45–58 percent. This example demonstrates the tremendously wide variations possible in the reserve ratio.

In those instances where the reserve ratio for the firm falls beneath the lower border of the appropriate range, the test may be utilized to justify a shorter life. However, there are cases when this situation is not important as a justification for a shorter taxable life, in view of the retirement and replacement practices of the taxpayer. As discussed earlier, new taxpayers, or a firm with a new guidelines class of assets, will necessarily have low reserve ratios; therefore this is not considered by the Treasury Department as meaningful until the guideline class has a history equal in years to the guideline life for that codification. Also, a low reserve ratio is not pertinent when the retirement or acquisition of assets results in a sudden and unusual decline in the ratio as compared to the preceding year as in the previous illustration.

But in those situations when the existence of a lower reserve ratio is meaningful and a shorter life is justifiable, a downward adjustment may be made in compliance with the rules of the *Revenue Procedure*. The range of adjustment is from 12.5 to 20 percent of the class life used in the preceding taxable year.

The foregoing example does not take into account some factors which complicate the application of the reserve-ratio test. For example, it assumes only the use of the straight-line method of depreciation while many firms use this method as well as the double-declining balance.

THE 1965 MODIFICATION IN TREASURY RULES FOR APPLICATION OF THE DEPRECIATION GUIDELINES

The three-year moratorium period provided for in connection with the new guidelines came to an end in 1965. This period, free of supervision from the Internal Revenue Service, was provided in order to allow the business community time to adjust its depreciation practices to the new guidelines before the reserve-ratio test would have to be met. However, as the 1965 deadline approached, it became increasingly apparent that many firms would not be able to meet the test. It was estimated that the inability of individual firms to meet the test in 1965 would have resulted in a $700 million reduction in depreciation charges.

The National Industrial Conference Board surveyed the depreciation practices of 273 firms and obtained information on the difficulties which individual firms expected to encounter in connection with passing the reserve-ratio test. The findings of the survey are presented in Table 26. It will be noted that only 14 percent of the firms surveyed would have been able to meet the test in 1965, and that 26.4 percent (72 firms) expected to fail the test by an amount in excess of 15 percentage points or more.

The principal problem with the new guidelines resulted from the fact that the reserve-ratio test tables assumed an even rate of growth and/or asset acquisition on the part of all business firms. This assumption was unrealistic since an even rate of asset acquisition proved to be the exception rather than the rule in actual business practice. Because capital investment proceeds at an irregular rate, investment in a given class of assets in any one year or group of years may be low or non-existent, causing the reserve ratio to tend toward the upper limit of its acceptable range or go below it. This problem, together with the objection of the business community in general that the three-year moratorium period was too short, brought about the 1965 modifications to the Treasury rules for the application of the depreciation guidelines.

The 1965 modifications extended the transitional period and allowed a more flexible reserve-ratio test in order to accommodate those firms which would not have been able to meet the test in 1965. The modifications included the "guideline form" and two transitional allowances. In addition,

TABLE 26

RESULTS OF A NATIONAL INDUSTRIAL CONFERENCE BOARD SURVEY OF 273 BUSINESSES REGARDING THEIR ABILITY TO MEET THE RESERVE-RATIO TEST IN 1965

Percentage Points of Expected Deviation*	Percentage of Adopters	
	1962	1965
−20 and Below	1.8	0
−19 to −15	2.2	1.1
−14 to −10	4.8	1.1
−9 to −5	8.8	1.8
−4 to −1	17.6	8.1
0	3.3	1.8
1 to 4	15.4	16.1
5 to 9	22.3	20.9
10 to 14	14.3	22.7
15 to 19	5.8	14.3
20 and Above	3.7	12.1

* Percentage points of expected deviation equals the actual reserve ratio, minus the appropriate upper limit. Minus signs, therefore, indicate the expected passing of the test.

one limiting change was made with respect to actual depreciation procedures.

The Guideline Form

The guideline form is intended to remedy the reserve-ratio tables. As they were originally constructed, they implicitly assumed an even rate of asset acquisition in any particular class, or in general. Each firm is compared to a norm which represents the average experience, and the firm which does not replace assets at regular intervals will often fail to meet the reserve-ratio test on this basis. In some years the depreciation reserve of such a firm increases while the cost factor is constant, resulting in an increase in the value of the ratio. The new guideline form allows such a firm to make allowances and adjustments suited to its particular pattern of asset acquisition, and thereby permits it to meet a reserve-ratio test which is tailored to its particular need.

To illustrate this problem more precisely, consider the instance of two firms which have had the same absolute rate of growth in any given asset class, but which have different patterns of asset acquisition. Assume both firms had assets of $100,000 in a given class during the base year. Over the next 10 years, taxpayer A acquired $10,000 worth of the same asset in each year, so that at the end of the tenth year, assets were $200,000. Taxpayer B, who also had $100,000 in the asset class during the base year, acquired $50,000 worth of the asset in year 1 and 2 of the time interval, so that at the end of the ten-year period he too had $200,000 in that asset class. Provided both firms used the same method of depreciation accounting, both would have had the same reserve ratio range to meet under the 1962 formulation of the reserve-ratio test. However, since the average age of the second firm's assets is greater, it would have accumulated a larger depreciation reserve, and therefore have a higher reserve ratio. It would often be the case that this reserve ratio would exceed the upper limit of the reserve-ratio range, since the original reserve-ratio table did not make provision for irregular growth patterns.

The guideline form is designed to eliminate this problem and to provide each taxpayer with an objective test suited to his individual pattern of asset acquisition. In order for a taxpayer to use the guideline form, he need only know the amount of assets purchased in any one class during the past year and in each of the previous years up to the length of the test life, plus 20 percent of the test life. The additional 20 percent when added to the test life gives the "extended test life," and is intended to provide the same flexibility in the guideline form that was present in the original reserve-ratio table which allowed the firm to hold on to an asset as much as 20 percent longer than its "useful" life and still meet the test (i.e., to use the guideline form the taxpayer working within any guideline class with a ten-year test life, must know the value of acquisition for a twelve-year period).

Under the guideline form, the taxpayer's actual reserve ratio (ratio of total depreciation deductions already taken on the assets in use to the original cost of the asset) is compared with the ratio limit which in turn is determined by dividing the total cost of assets purchased during the extended life for that particular class of assets into the total "computed" reserve for that period.

$$\text{Reserve-Ratio Limit} = \frac{\text{Total Computed Reserve}}{\text{Total Cost of Assets}}$$

If the actual reserve ratio is equal to or less than the reserve-ratio limit, the firm has passed the test and may continue to use the new guidelines.

The "computed" reserve is calculated by multiplying the cost of assets for each year by an annual factor which is provided in the guideline form table of annual factors given by the Treasury Department. These annual factors are provided for assets of all test lives and for each method of

TABLE 27
THE WORKING OF THE GUIDELINE FORM

Year	Cost of Assets	Annual Factors	Computed Reserve
1954	$25,000	1.000	$25,000
1955	10,000	1.000	10,000
1956	35,000	.950	33,250
1957	30,000	.850	25,500
1958	35,000	.750	26,250
1959	15,000	.650	9,750
1960	20,000	.550	11,000
1961	15,000	.450	6,750
1962	25,000	.350	8,750
1963	30,000	.250	7,500
1964	20,000	.150	3,000
1965	35,000	.050	1,750
Total	$295,000		$168,500

$$\text{Res. Ratio Limit} = \frac{\text{Computed Reserve}}{\text{Total Cost}} = \frac{168,500}{295,000} = 57.12$$

depreciation accounting. The cost of assets in each year is simply the gross original cost exclusive of any depreciation charges.

The following example illustrates the working of the guideline form. It will be assumed the taxpayer is in the year 1965 and is working with assets with a a test life of 10 years and an extended life of 12 years (i.e. extended life = test life + 20 percent). The depreciation accounting method will be the straight-line method. Recall that if the extended life is 12 years, the taxpayer must have the cost of assets acquired in each of the last 12 years, or in this instance back to 1954. These asset costs for the respective years are given in column 2 of Table 27. The annual factors taken from the factor table are in column 3, and the computed reserve, col. 2 times col. 3, is given in column 4.

Provided that the firm in question had an actual reserve ratio of 57.12 or less, it would meet the reserve-ratio test for that class of assets. The guideline form, as illustrated above, is an alternate method available to the taxpayer to meet the reserve-ratio limit. It has not replaced the reserve-ratio table, nor does it prevent a firm from using the reserve-ratio tables for other classes of assets. The taxpayer is also free to substitute one system for the other from year to year according to his needs. In most instances, the most beneficial system will depend upon the pattern of asset acquisition. When a large part of the assets purchased in any class is concentrated in the early years of the extended life, the guideline form will provide a higher reserve-ratio limit. Conversely, when asset acquisition is concentrated in the latter years of the extended life, the reserve-ratio table will generally yield a higher limit.

Transitional Rules

In order to cope with the second major difficulty associated with the 1962 formulation of the depreciation guidelines, namely the relatively short period of adjustment, two additional transitional rules were introduced in 1965. They are a "Transitional Allowance Rule" and a "Minimal Adjustment Rule," both of which are intended to accommodate those firms which would not have been able to meet the reserve-ratio test in 1965.

(A) *The Transitional-Allowance Rule.* Under the transitional-allowance rule a firm will be judged to have met the reserve-ratio test in the fourth taxable year so long as its actual reserve ratio does not exceed the upper limit of the reserve-ratio test by more than 15 percentage points. The extra 15 points allowance may be added to the upper limit of the standard reserve-ratio range or to the upper limit of the guideline form, depending on the individual taxpayer's preference.

During the first year, the transitional allowance will be set at 15 percentage points, but in the following years will decline at a given rate depending on the "transitional life" which is generally equal to the test life of a given asset. During the first half of this period, one-third of the allowance of 5 percentage points will be eliminated, and in the second half of the period the remaining two-thirds will be consumed. For instance, given an asset with a test life of 10 years, the rate at which the 15-point allowance would decline is as follows: during the first half of the period (5 years) one point per year would be removed such that at the end of the five-year period 5 percentage points would have been accounted for.

During the second 5 years, 2 points per year will be deducted so that at the end of the full ten-year period, the entire 15 percentage points will be consumed.

The incorporation of the transitional-allowance rule will not prevent individual firms from using the trending rule as provided for in the 1962 formulation. However, the transitional-allowance rule is not to be used for the purposes of applying the trending rule, and as was provided for in the 1962 formulation, once the trending-rule test has been failed, it may not be used again. The transitional-allowance rule, however, is available for use during the entire transitional period. The transitional-allowance rule is of particular benefit for those firms which desired to take advantage of the revised guidelines but found the three-year moratorium too short a period to bring their actual depreciation practices into line with the limits set by the reserve-ratio test. With the added allowance provided by the rule, it is felt that most firms should be able to meet the reserve-ratio test or the guideline form.

(B) *The Minimal Adjustment Rule.* The second transitional rule, the minimal adjustment rule, is directed at those firms which are unable to meet the reserve-ratio test or the guideline form even with the additional transitional allowance. Formerly, a firm which was unable to meet the test or at least the trending rule, was subject to an adjustment in the asset lives not to exceed 25 percent of the life. Under the minimal adjustment rule, the life may be extended by only 5 or 10 percent depending on the circumstances peculiar to the individual firm. For instance, should the actual reserve ratio exceed the upper limit of the transition limit by less than 10 points, the asset life may be increased by not more than 5 percent. If the transition limit is exceeded by more than 10 points, the asset life may be extended by no more than 10 percent of the original life. Under the minimal-adjustment rule, the asset life is extended according to the scale mentioned above for the year of failure. When an adjustment is made in one year, no further adjustment can be made in the next year. However, if failure persists in subsequent years, additional adjustments may be made in order to bring actual depreciation practices into line with the life of the assets as stipulated in the depreciation guidelines.

Limit on Depreciation Procedures

Aside from the 1965 changes in the depreciation guidelines which have been mentioned thus far, one additional and limiting change was also included. This change is intended to prevent exaggerated depreciation deductions taken under the new guidelines resulting from the use of open-end, multiple asset accounts in conjunction with the straight-line and sum of the year's digits depreciation accounting methods. In order to eliminate the exaggerated depreciation deductions, firms will not be able to use the guideline procedure starting in 1965, unless the cost of each year's assets are listed in a yearly acquisition account or in item accounts. This qualification applies only to those firms using the straight-line or sum of the year's digits accounting methods with open-end, multiple asset accounts.

REVALUATION PROPOSALS

The purpose of revaluation is to compensate for the declining value of the dollar caused by inflation. Revaluation proposals would permit assets to be revalued by the application of a suitable price or cost index which would allow the taxpayer to recover the purchasing power of the original dollars invested and so help reduce the gap between the amount of depreciation allowed and actual replacement costs. In these proposals no attempt is made to recover the full replacement cost of the asset, but rather the purchasing power of the dollars originally involved in the acquisition of the facility to be replaced. Thus, just as cost of living adjustments permit the wage earner to maintain his purchasing power, so revaluation allows the investor to do the same.

One plan advanced would apply a procedure whereby a company's total plant would be revalued each year on the basis of a price index. The rate of depreciation would not be changed. The price index, if desirable, could be specifically computed for the industry in question; or a more general index might be applied. For example, if a company had depreciable property valued at $1,000,000 in 1961 and the price index showed an advance of 2 percent in 1962, the company's property would be revalued at $1,020,000 which amount would also be depreciated at 5 percent. In the next year if the index increased another 2 percent, the property value would increase to $1,040,000 on which the regular 5 percent depreciation would be taken. In this way the total real cost of the annual wear and tear on capital equipment would be recovered each year.

This plan presupposes, but does not demand, that the additional depreciation charged be reinvested. If put into practice, it would work in both inflationary and deflationary periods; for when the price index declines, the value of plant and equipment would be reduced as would be the amount of depreciation charged off each year.

A second plan which has been advanced was incorporated in a bill— H.R. 131—introduced in 1961 by Representative Keogh of New York and in a similar bill introduced by Senator Hartke of Indiana. The method is somewhat similar to the first proposal discussed insofar as it permits the revaluation of depreciable property on the basis of a price index. But it differs in certain respects. The property is not revalued until it is to be replaced. At that time an acceptable index would be applied, and the value of the asset would be expressed in terms of current dollars. The difference between the original cost and the current value of the asset is then taken as a deduction before taxes, provided that the total amount, that is, the original cost plus the differential, is reinvested in the business.

The proposal also permits the company to spread this additional depreciation deduction over a three-year period, for it is quite possible that the deduction of an exceptionally large sum in any one year would affect the profit and loss statement too drastically in that year.

A concrete example will illustrate the method: If in 1940 a firm installed an asset with a twenty-year life at a cost of $100,000, it should be replaced in 1959 or 1960. By that time, $100,000 would have been charged off as depreciation under the tax laws and the original cost recovered. However the purchasing power of the 1960 dollar is approximately half that of its 1940 counterpart, or, in other terms, the $100,000 investment made then would be the equivalent of $200,000 in 1960. According to the proposal, the company would be permitted to charge off to depreciation in the year of replacement an extra $100,000 to adjust for the loss due to inflation. The total, namely, $200,000, must be reinvested in new assets.

It would not be necessary, however, to replace the identical asset; another type of asset could be bought, provided the entire $200,000 was expended. For example, the facility in question might have been used for drawing steel wire. With strong foreign competition existing in this particular field, the company might feel that it was no longer a profitable operation and instead might spend the $200,000 involved for a facility that would roll steel strip. But the objective of the proposal would still be achieved; the additional depreciation plus the original depreciation would be invested to modernize the firm's plant and also help to create jobs in the production of the new facilities.

Revaluation proposals have often been criticized on the grounds that a satisfactory price index cannot be computed. It is claimed that any index which is calculated will prove to be too complicated or else too imprecise to be of practical use in the revaluation of productive assets. Without going into the technicalities of price indices, it is not clear why a reasonably serviceable one could not be obtained. In fact, indices such as the well known consumer price index are constantly in use at the present time and are generally accepted as guides in important fields such as labor negotiations. It seems likely that the construction of an index suitable for use in asset revaluation would not involve significantly more serious problems than those which have already been overcome in the consumer price index.

Finally, there is no reason why a suitable index should not be used for asset revaluation even if, as may well be the case, it cannot be computed with extreme precision. By refusing to permit asset revaluation on the grounds that an exact index of prices cannot be computed, we are relying by default upon a much less precise index—one which demands that depreciation be calculated on the assumption that prices are not changing at all.

INVESTMENT INCENTIVES

The distinction between depreciation reform and investment incentives is a significant one. Both perform very useful, but by no means identical, functions. The former is a means of providing sufficient funds for the modernization and replacement of plant and equipment, and if carried out should be built permanently into the tax structure. The latter can be designed to act as a stimulant for modernization or expansion and can become a permanent part of the tax structure. This device has been used frequently abroad as is indicated in the section on foreign tax laws where a number of investment incentives were discussed.

The Administration proposed a tax incentive as part of its overall tax program. In his 1961 message, President Kennedy stated:

Specifically, therefore, I recommend enactment of an investment tax incentive in the form of a tax credit of
. . . 15 percent of all new plant and equipment investment expenditures in excess of current depreciation allowances.
. . . 6 percent of such expenditures below this level but in excess of 50 percent of depreciation allowances; with
. . . 10 percent on the first $5,000 of new investment as a minimum credit. This credit would be taken as an offset against the firm's tax liability, up to an overall limitation of 30 percent in the reduction of that liability in any one year. It would be separate from and in addition to depreciation of the eligible new investment at cost. It would be available to individually owned businesses as well as corporate enterprises, and apply to eligible investment expenditures made after January 1 of this year. To remain a real incentive and make a maximum contribution to those areas of capital expansion and modernization where it is most needed, and to permit efficient administration, eligible investment expenditures would be limited to expenditures on new plant and equipment, and on assets with a life of six years or more.[5]

This proposal, as the message states, was designed to make a contribution in the area of capital expansion as well as modernization. Thus it was not limited to replacement and in that sense was not exclusively depreciation reform. Further, it did not attempt to solve the problem of erosion of capital due to inflation.

The original proposal of the Administration made in April 1961 was modified in a bill (H.R. 10650), "The Revenue Act of 1962," introduced in the House of Representatives on March 12, 1962. A brief summary of this bill as introduced states:

... that a business can subtract from its tax liability 8 percent of its new investment in tangible business assets other than buildings. This tax credit is an outright subtraction from the tax and is in addition to the full allowable depreciation of the cost of the asset. The amount of the credit that can be taken in any year is limited by the amount of tax. The limitation involves the figure of $100,000 of tax liability. For a taxpayer whose tax (before the credit) is not over $100,000, the credit can offset his tax dollar for dollar. Where the tax is larger than $100,000, the credit is limited to $100,000 plus 50 percent of the part of the tax over $100,000. Any dollar amount of credit which is not usable (because of this limitation based on the tax) may be carried over and used against tax of the following 5 years.

Amendment to this Bill, adopted prior to its passage by the House on March 29, 1962, reduced the $100,000 figure to $25,000 and the 50 percent of the part of taxes over $100,000 to 25 percent. Further, the 8 percent credit was reduced to 7 percent.

Among other proposed investment incentives was the Increased Initial Write-Off which involved the extension and liberalization of the special initial allowances adopted in 1958 as an anti-recession benefit for small business. The 1958 measure provided that during the first year after the acquisition of an asset, a firm can deduct, over and above normal depreciation, an additional write-off of 20 percent of the purchase price of equipment totaling $10,000. The Increased Initial Write-Off proposal would lift this $10,000 ceiling. If the ceiling were lifted to one million dollars, for example, this would give the firm spending that much for equipment an additional write-off of $200,000 above the regular depreciation allowance for the first year.

Another incentive proposed by Representative Wright Patman of Texas involved a temporary increase in depreciation allowances. It would permit business men to deduct, in the year of acquisition, 100 percent of the cost of capital equipment acquired up to a maximum of $500,000. This increase in allowances had a time limit so that after 1962 depreciation write-offs would have been restored to this previous status. A proposal of this nature would be useful as a temporary measure but would be of little-long-term value unless extended from time to time. Even if so extended it would suffer from the defect of introducing a substantial element of uncertainty into business planning unless enacted on a permanent basis. The same criticism can be made of investment incentive proposals in general insofar as they are regarded as "one-shot" measures or as purely anti-recessionary devices.

The four approaches which touch in some manner or another on the problem of depreciation: (1) expedients for making up deficiencies; (2) adjustment of the useful life of an asset; (3) revaluation of an asset to compensate for the declining value of the dollar due to inflation; and (4) tax incentives, all have varying effects in terms of a solution of the problem. The expedients which involve borrowing and the sale of stock are strictly emergency measures and of little help as a permanent solution. The reinvestment of retained earnings has in practice been frequently employed, but again this is an expedient of dubious long-term desirability.

The necessity of using profits to pay for the replacement of assets tends to raise prices and may lead to a paradox in which the firm is subsidizing its consumers by earning an inadequate rate of profit and yet is charging higher prices than would be necessary if realistic depreciation allowances were permitted. Finally, inadequate depreciation allowances for the replacement of existing equipment which result in phantom profits and unnecessary price increases also can easily lead to improper decisions on new investments. The decision to expand or not to expand existing capacity can be no better than the information on which it is based. If the basic price and profit data are distorted, investment decisions based on them are also likely to be ill-founded. This in turn can produce undesirable distortions and fluctuations in the economy.

The measures that deal with shortening useful lives and the revaluation of assets get to the heart of the problem. Provision for the former has been made and if this revision were to be coupled with an allowance for inflation, much would be done to solve the problem of obsolescence by encouraging the modernization of plant and equipment.

The revision of useful lives contained in *Revenue Procedure 62–21* has several objectives: to simplify the depreciation codes; to increase the cash flow of corporations; to encourage industrial modernization and thus stimulate economic growth at home and enable American firms to compete more successfully abroad. According to the U.S. Department of Commerce, corporate depreciation allowances in 1962 increased by $4.1 billion of which $2.4 billion was attributable to the useful lives revision. The tax credit provided over $1 billion.[6] Table 28 outlines the results of the 1962 tax changes on an industry basis.

The impact of the guideline changes varied substantially from industry to industry. Whereas the new guidelines resulted in additions to deprecia-

TABLE 28

DEPRECIATION DEDUCTIONS, BY GUIDELINE AND NONGUIDELINE USE, AND INVESTMENT TAX CREDIT, ALL CORPORATIONS, 1962
(Millions of dollars)

	1960	1961	Corporate Depreciation 1962			Additional Depreciation from Guideline Use	1962 Investment Tax Credit
			Total	Using Guidelines	Not Using Guidelines		
All corporations	22,160	23,577	27,708	14,771	12,937	2,431	1,041
Manufacturing and mining	10,559	11,202	13,623	9,323	4,300	1,723	516
Food and beverage	965	1,016	1,234	745	489	119	58
Textile	319	353	425	245	180	38	20
Paper	466	511	673	586	87	121	25
Chemical	1,154	1,266	1,562	1,380	182	263	68
Petroleum refining and extraction	1,739	1,803	2,055	1,223	832	166	45
Rubber	214	237	300	178	122	30	16
Stone, clay and glass	460	482	599	386	213	92	29
Metal refining and extraction	1,188	1,228	1,590	1,288	302	287	61
Iron and steel manufacturing	661	NA	899	813	86	182	27
Machinery except electrical	860	926	1,130	532	598	75	30
Electrical machinery	478	528	628	489	139	71	24
Motor vehicles and parts	713	721	870	841	29	149	32
Transportation equipment excluding motor vehicles	255	254	245	90	155	14	10
Other manufacturing and mining	1,748	1,877	2,312	1,340	972	298	98
Transportation	1,942	2,066	2,557	1,481	1,076	365	102
Public utilities	2,220	2,395	2,621	1,279	1,342	104	103
Communication	1,084	1,199	1,334	210	1,124	11	75
Commercial and other	6,355	6,715	7,573	2,478	5,095	228	245

Source: U.S. Department of Commerce, Office of Business Economics.

tion write-offs of 17 percent in transportation and 14 percent in mining, increased depreciation charges for guideline users in public utilities and the commercial group were less than 10 percent higher than their charges on the old basis.

Of particular interest in determining the success of the new guidelines is the fact that only 54.5 percent of the corporations surveyed by the Commerce Department made use of the revised lives. Indications are that small and medium-sized firms have not made use of the guidelines to the same extent as larger businesses. According to the Commerce Department, the increase in depreciation for large firms (assets over $100 million) was 18 percent of 1962 deductions on a pre-guideline basis; for small firms the increase was 7 percent and for medium-sized firms, 15 percent. The small and medium-sized category consisted of firms with assets of under $10 million.

A number of firms, particularly smaller businesses, hesitated to make use of the new guidelines because of difficulties surrounding the reserve-ratio test. This led to the 1965 modifications of the tax law which extended the transition period and provided the guideline form and two transitional allowances to accomodate those having difficulty with the reserve-ratio test. However, the reserve ratio has been retained as a part of the tax structure. Further, the new guideline rules are not permanent but may be rescinded by Treasury decision, a fact which many consider even more prohibitive to their adoption than the reserve-ratio test.

A solution to these problems, Amendment 319 to H.R. 8363, has been introduced by Sentator Hartke of Indiana and co-sponsored by Senator Javits of New York. It makes the guideline lives permanent matters of right rather than administrative procedures which can be cancelled upon Treasury decision and eliminates the complicated reserve-ratio test. Under the proposed amendment, the Secretary of the Treasury would issue regulations describing classes of tangible property and prescribe a useful life with respect to each class not longer than the lives established in *Revenue Procedure 62–21*. At his option, the taxpayer could then use these lives to compute his depreciation deductions without regard to his replacement policy on the assets being depreciated. This would make it possible for taxpayers to use the guideline lives without the limitations currently imposed by the reserve-ratio test now contained in *Revenue Procedure 62–21*.

The first plan offered for asset revaluation, viz., the application year-by-year of a price index, has the useful feature of permitting a company to write off less depreciation should there be a deflationary trend in the economy. Thus, taxes and earnings would tend to be stabilized in both

I

inflationary and deflationary periods. This proposal would permit companies to protect themselves against changes in the replacement cost of their capital assets in a manner analogous to the way in which they have been protected against fluctuations in the value of their inventories since the introduction of the Last-In, First-Out method of inventory accounting by the Treasury Department in 1938.[7]

The second revaluation plan, the Keogh and Hartke Bills, would permit a realistic charge for wear and tear on capital and could take care of past deficiencies, as well as those that might occur in the future. The requirement to reinvest the entire allowance also means that any loss of income-tax revenues from the plan will be minimized. In connection with the need for revaluation, it must be remembered that many firms will continue to suffer the effects of past inflation in inadequate depreciation allowances for many years even if no more inflation were to occur. Hence, revaluation would remain desirable even if prices were to remain stable in the future.

The investment tax credit plan which became law in 1962 was designed to stimulate investment not only for replacement but also for expansion. This was achieved successfully in regard to replacement, for more funds were available to modernize plant and equipment. After 1963 there was also a considerable expansion in capital investment as expenditure for plant and equipment increased to $44.9 billion in 1964, 14.5 percent higher than the 1963 outlay. This sharp upward trend continued in 1965 with an increase of 15.8 percent over 1964. A comparable increase was posted for 1966.

The tax credit was not the only factor responsible for the expansion which took place. There were other non-tax stimulants to investments operating during this period, particularly the increased demand for goods and services throughout the economy from accelerated activity in Vietnam.

A difficulty with the 7 percent tax credit is that it could be rendered ineffective in the case of some firms because of the ceiling put on the amount of dollars which can be deducted from taxes. The law, as amended, requires that the total number of dollars be no more than $25,000 plus 25 percent of the total tax bill over and above this initial $25,000, so that if a firm earned $1 million *after* taxes, then its tax bill, with a 52 percent tax rate, would also be approximately $1 million. It would be permitted under the amended version of the law to take a maximum tax credit of $275,000 to $280,000. While this might be helpful, it is quite possible that a firm in this category could spend $8 to $10 million annually on capital investments, and 7 percent of this would be $560,000 to $700,000. Here, in effect, the firm is not getting a 7 percent tax credit on total new capital investments; on expenditures of $10 million, the tax credit would be less than 3 percent.

There are a number of firms in this category, which although not small, are definitely marginal in their industry. In many instances they are marginal because they lack modern equipment. The intent of the change in the law is to help these firms but, in effect, they will receive little aid. It is true that the law permits this credit to be carried forward for five years. However, there is little prospect that such a company can increase its profits substantially and thus the credit will remain approximately the same, while on the other hand it must spend amounts at least equal to its depreciation charges in order to maintain its facilities. Seven percent of such expenditure will always be far in excess of the credit granted. Thus, unfortunately, the marginal firms in large industries who need help most are helped little by the tax incentive plan. They are marginal frequently because their equipment, or at least part of their equipment, is obsolete and they often have difficulty in obtaining the necessary financing to rectify the situation. The limitation section of the tax incentive program in these instances tends to limit the hoped-for effects of the law.

This was unfortunate enough, but an amendment was added to the bill as it passed the Senate which limited the tax credit even further. This amendment remained in force for a year and a half until it was repealed by the Revenue Act of 1964. Any loss incurred due to the amendment was compensated for by future tax credits so that no refunds were made. This amendment dealt with adjustments to the base value of the property. Under Section 48G it stated:

In General—the basis of any section 38 property shall be reduced, for purposes of this subtitle other than this subpart, by an amount equal to 7 percent of the qualified investment as determined under Section 46(c) with respect to such property.

This meant that it was necessary to reduce the value of any property acquired for which tax credit was taken by 7 percent, or the full value of the tax credit. Thus, for depreciation purposes an asset was valued at 7 percent less than the amount for which it was acquired. This had the effect of reducing the 7 percent tax credit to $3\frac{1}{2}$ percent over the depreciable lifetime of the asset.

An example will help to clarify this point. If a piece of equipment is purchased for $100,000, the firm is allowed 7 percent, or $7,000 against its tax liability. However, the $7,000 must be deducted from the value of the asset so that the depreciable base is reduced to $93,000. If we assume that this particular piece of equipment has a ten-year life and we further assume a straight-line basis for depreciation, the asset is written off at $9,300 a year so that at the end of 10 years in place of writing off $100,000, which was the original cost, only $93,000 is charged against depreciation before taxes. The $7,000 which has been deducted from the base value cannot be charged against depreciation and thus it must be put into profits where it is taxed at 50 percent (if present rates are applied for a large company) so that the firm pays $3,500. Thus it would have the $93,000 accrued to depreciation, plus $3,500 after taxes, which would be $96,500. Although $7,000 of the original $100,000 is granted at the outset in the form of a tax credit and the firm has the use of this money, it must pay back $3,500 in taxes over the life-span of the asset. This, in effect, reduced the tax credit of 7 percent to $3\frac{1}{2}$ percent and limited the effectiveness of the bill to some degree.

THE EFFECT OF REFORMS AND INCENTIVES IN TAX REVENUES

One of the principal objections to proposals for depreciation reform has been a concern over the cost of these proposals in terms of tax revenue. Much of this concern stems from the fact that depreciation reform is often regarded as a tax giveaway. If, for example, additional depreciation were allowed on a national scale in the amount of 5 billion dollars, it is maintained that with a 50 percent tax rate the taxpayers who receive this allowance would pay 2.5 billion dollars less in income tax. This seems to be the case at first sight, but actually it is only the beginning of a process wherein a number of offsetting sources of additional tax revenue would be activated.

Both depreciation reform and tax incentives encourage investment in productive plant and equipment; in the former instance for replacement and modernization and in the latter instance for expansion of existing capacity as well as replacement. This is particularly true of reinvestment depreciation which requires that the full amount of the accrued depreciation and the total additional allowance be invested in new machinery and equipment. However, in view of the large proportion of obsolete facilities at the present time, it is probable that most of the additional depreciation allowed under the various other proposed reforms and revisions would also be reinvested. Under the circumstances, the economic effects of these proposals would be substantially the same as those of reinvestment depreciation.

If a given amount of money is invested in machinery and equipment, the expenditures necessary at each stage in the production of this equipment from the processing of raw materials through to the final assembly generate payments for wages, materials, and service, as well as income from sales. All of these items furnish a basis for income tax. The typical sales dollar of the capital goods producers, particularly those who produce heavy long-lived machinery, has been broken down into materials, labor, and other items. On the basis of this breakdown, using the lowest tax rate now in force on personal income, a conservative computation was made of the amount of tax revenue which would be generated by expenditures made on productive depreciable property. It was found that for each $100 spent on machinery and equipment about $26 of tax revenue was generated.[8]

Of a given $100 invested in machinery, $55 is expended for materials, supplies, and services, $35 for wages and the remaining $10 is profit before taxes. From the wages paid, the Government collects 20 percent, or $7 in income taxes. On the equipment firm's profit of $10, the corporation income tax is 50 percent, or $5.00. Thus, the total tax revenue from the activities of the primary manufacturer amounts to $12.00. Suppliers of the equipment manufacturer incur total material costs of $30.25 and wage costs of $19.25. Their profits before tax amount to $5.50. Income taxes on wages and profits amount to $3.85 and $2.75 respectively, a total of $6.60. Taking all other tiers of suppliers as a group, wage costs total $27.22 and company profits $3.03, resulting in personal income taxes of $5.45 and corporate income taxes of $1.52. Thus, the activity stimulated by the investment in productive capacity of $100 ultimately generates, on the average, $25.57 in income taxes.

Given the fact that each $100 spent on productive plant and equipment generates $26 in tax revenues, it can be seen from the following detailed example that any loss of tax revenue which might result from a change in the depreciation laws will in all probability be quite small. The ABC Company which bought a machine for $1,000 in 1940 is about to retire it in 1962 and discovers that its replacement cost is $2,500. Under reinvestment depreciation, the firm is eligible to recoup the purchasing power of the $1,000 investment made in 1940 in terms of 1962 dollars. This is approximately two 1962 dollars for each 1940 dollar so that an additional $1,000 can be written off before taxes. Under these circumstances, the loss to the Government in tax revenues, assuming a 50 percent tax rate, would be $500. However, $2,500 is spent to replace the asset. On the basis of $26 worth of taxes accruing to the Treasury for every $100 spent, the Government would collect $650, a net gain of $150. Some might object that the replacement cost figure of $2,500 is too high. However, experience has shown that the typical replacement of prewar assets in recent years has been at 2 to $2\frac{1}{2}$ times the original cost.

The argument is often advanced that the original $1,000 in accrued depreciation would be spent anyway since most companies ordinarily reinvest their full depreciation allowance. Thus we can only calculate the added revenue to the Government on the basis of the additional $1,500 which is in excess of the accrued depreciation. In this case, on the expenditure of the $1,500 the Government would collect $390 in taxes which would represent a deficit of $110 in revenue as a result of asset revaluation. The supposition that the $1,000 of accrued depreciation would be spent even if not supplemented is by no means a valid one, for quite a number of companies have continued to operate obsolete equipment when adequate funds were not available to modernize. Hence, their accrued depreciation has not been fully spent; and these companies have incurred higher costs in their operations, have earned lower profits and have paid lower taxes. Further, in the long run, tax reforms and incentives which encourage modern techniques of production can bring about cost reductions and higher profit levels thus broadening the tax base and generating additional revenue. This has been demonstrated by the experience of Canada where depreciation write-offs, corporate profits and corporate income collections have all grown rapidly since the introduction of liberalized depreciation in the late 1940s.[9] It can also be observed with respect to many companies that have installed a considerable amount of modern equipment during the past 10 years. A number of these have been able to improve their earnings as a result of more efficient operations due to modern facilities. The opposite has been true of other firms who, because of their inability to invest adequately in plant and equipment, have shown either very poor earnings or actual losses at low rates of operation.

In connection with possible revenue losses resulting from depreciation reform which would permit a more accurate statement of profits, it should be pointed out that the Government has long recognized the undesirable effects of overstating profits. In two situations, viz., the increase in the value of business inventories and private homes, protection has been given against the effects of inflation.

Since 1938 businesses have been protected from profit and tax distortions arising from changes in the value of their inventories as a result of the decision of the Treasury Department to allow them to use the well-known LIFO (Last-In, First-Out) method in determining their taxable profits. This system is based upon recognition of the fact that while a company may realize a book profit on the sale of an item at a higher price than its cost because of inflation, no real profit has actually been made (or should be taxed) until the item has been replaced in inventory at the current cost. The use of LIFO accounting enables companies to squeeze the "phantom" profits out of their taxable income by calculating their profits on the assumption that the last item sold was also the most recent (and highest cost) item added to inventory. The use of the LIFO system during the inflationary post-World War II period has enabled companies which must maintain large investments in inventories to avoid serious problems of overstated profits, arbitrary taxation and insufficient after-tax revenues to maintain the productive integrity of the business. Companies which must maintain large investments in capital assets and which cannot take advantage of the LIFO method have been much less able to avoid these problems.

Similarly, in 1951 Congress amended the tax laws to provide that a homeowner who sells his house at a profit need pay no tax on the profit if he reinvests it in another house within a year. Congress recognized in effect that the homeowner receives no gain in real terms on the disposition of his dwelling at a profit resulting from inflation because the purchase of a home of equal quality would cost him an equal amount of money. Hence to tax the profit arising from the sale of his home would be to tax arbitrarily the increased money value of his home resulting from inflation. A tax upon the homeowner's book profit would reduce the amount of real funds available for the purchase of a new dwelling. This would compel him to buy a new home of lesser quality than the one he sold unless he supplements the after-tax selling price with funds of his own. This situation, which Congress changed the law to prevent, is analogous to the difficulty facing many businesses which must use profits in order to replace capital assets purchased at, and depreciated on, the basis of the much lower prices of 20 years ago.

Congress long ago recognized and halted the taxation of "phantom" profits resulting from increases in the value of inventories and private houses because of inflation. It seems proper that Congress should similarly recognize and halt the taxation of phantom profits resulting from inadequate depreciation allowances for capital assets in times of inflation. This necessity is underlined by the present urgent need to reduce costs, create new jobs, increase productivity, and maintain the position of the United States in world markets.

In the President's 1961 tax message to Congress it was estimated that the tax credit plan, described as an incentive for "the modernization and expansion of private plant and equipment," would cost the Treasury some 1.7 billion dollars in revenue. On the other hand, it was also stated that "economic expansion . . . creates a growing tax base, thus increasing revenue . . . " and that the tax credit plan would "generate increased demand, raise overall economic activity, and create 500,000 new jobs."[10]

If it can be assumed that the annual income from each of these jobs is between $4,000 and $5,000 a year, the aggregate amount of new income generated would be between 2 and 2.5 billion dollars. Personal income taxes on this amount, as well as the additional corporate income taxes generated by a higher level of business activity, would do much to offset the estimated 1.7 billion dollar revenue loss. In fact, it is quite conceivable that the deficit would be eliminated completely. Thus it seems that depreciation revision of the tax credit variety, as well as other incentives and reforms, is capable of generating considerable income and should cost the Treasury little, if anything, in tax revenues.

OPINIONS ON DEPRECIATION REFORM

Although informed opinion for the most part has been in favor of changes in the depreciation-tax structure, a number of objections to this kind of tax revision have been raised. Some of these arguments have already been treated indirectly as various aspects of the general discussion on depreciation. It seems appropriate, however, that they be considered separately and in detail for a more complete understanding of the problem.

LOSS OF TAX REVENUE

Some contend that higher depreciation allowances mean lower tax payments and would result in a loss of tax revenue. The effects of an increase in depreciation allowances upon tax revenues have already been discussed. The conclusion that higher allowances will lead only to a loss in tax revenues does not take into account the complete impact which will be experienced once adequate funds for the maintenance and replacement of plant and equipment are made available to industry.

The effects of adequate depreciation allowances could well be beneficial to the Treasury, for once funds to make up the deficiency between replacement costs and depreciation are made available, investment will increase and, in fact, has increased as previously neglected replacements take place. Further, taxable incomes (payments for materials, services and labor) earned in the production of the required facilities will increase, and the additional tax revenues derived from these sources will materially help to offset the initial reduction in revenue resulting from increased allowances. In the long run, the installation of modern facilities will also act to increase efficiency and reduce costs, thereby broadening the tax base and again increasing revenues.

Finally, if depreciation allowances are inadequate for the replacement of capital, then capital, rather than the income derived from its use, becomes a source of taxation and this results in at least a partial confiscation of assets.

REINVESTMENT

Concern has been expressed in some quarters that even though depreciation reform makes funds available, it does not guarantee that they will be expended. The confusion over the effect of increased depreciation charges on the revenues stems largely from this objection which overlooks a significant aspect of a comprehensive, well-formulated depreciation reform policy. Under reinvestment depreciation the additional allowance equal to the difference between an asset's historical cost and its inflated replacement cost is permitted to be deducted only if both amounts (the accrued historical cost and the added allowance) are reinvested in productive facilities. Consequently, a firm would not be allowed to liquidate its assets and at the same time collect the additional allowance provided to offset inflation. The reinvestment of the funds acquired under any proposed tax revision is essential to the maintenance of the level of tax revenues.

FAVORITISM TO LARGE FIRMS

There are some critics of depreciation reform who fear that increased allowances for depreciation favor large firms with substantial capital structures rather than small firms. It must be admitted that the total amount of depreciation written off by a firm which employs a large aggregate of capital equipment is naturally greater than the total for a firm which requires limited amounts of productive equipment. The depreciation charges of such a firm are greater because the costs incurred in capital erosion are greater. When governed by the prescribed useful lives as established in the tax law, write-offs per unit of physical capital are equal regardless of the amount of depreciable property in operation and total write-offs are proportional to the amount of depreciable property. If depreciation reform results in any special or exclusive benefit, it appears that small business enterprises have the most to gain since it would reduce their dependence on outside sources of capital as a means for the replacement of facilities. Small firms are often at a decided disadvantage in relation to larger companies when it is necessary to obtain replacement funds through borrowing.

RELATION TO CAPITAL MARKET

Some have expressed the opinion that depreciation allowances reduce competitive forces in the capital market. This view stems from a misunderstanding of the concept and function of depreciation. If depreciation reserves are considered as a means for capital expansion, it could be argued correctly that they subvert free competitive forces in the capital market. This would be a perfectly valid argument, for a legitimate means to corporate expansion is through competition in the sale of stock or in direct borrowing. Expansion, however, is not the object of depreciation. The purpose of depreciation is to account for one of the important costs of doing business, namely, the gradual wear and tear on productive facilities. The funds it provides for the replacement of equipment, like funds for wages or the cost of materials, are correctly obtained, not from the capital markets, but from internal sources.

The long-run unsuitability of borrowing and the sale of stock as sources of funds to replace equipment and machinery have already been treated in the discussion of the various supplements to inadequate depreciation reserves. In order to provide for capital replacement which generally occurs every year, borrowing would be an annual event which could eventually result in bankruptcy. Likewise, the sale of stock would not provide a legitimate source of funds for replacement since it dilutes, without compensation, the stockholders' equity, both in their investment and in the company's earnings.

INCREASE IN STOCKHOLDERS' EQUITY THROUGH INFLATION

It has been advanced that depreciation reform is unwarranted because the value of the stockholders' equity in the business increases as inflation occurs. It is claimed that the shareholders are compensated for the gap between depreciation allowances and replacement costs resulting from inflation by an increase in the value of the business as a whole. This argument fails to meet the problem of depreciation reform for two reasons. First, the value of the business has probably not risen in real terms because of inflation, so the stockholders are actually no better and no worse off than before in this respect. Second, this reasoning does not meet the basic difficulty of inadequate depreciation allowances, namely, that the funds provided by depreciation are insufficient to pay for the replacement of assets when current costs are higher than at the time of acquisition.

RELATION TO RESEARCH AND DEVELOPMENT

The concern that increased depreciation allowances may depress economic growth by encouraging investment in plant and equipment at the expense of research and development expenditures has been expressed by some. This argument is not essentially valid, for under an acceptable method of depreciation reform, funds could and should be earmarked for the replacement of productive plant and equipment. As such, these funds serve a definite and necessary business function and cannot be used for other purposes such as research and development. Wage payments and materials purchases are also necessary costs of production (and thus are similar to depreciation allowances which account for capital cost), but no one would argue that wages and the cost of materials *per se* discourage research and development activity.

Depreciation allowances and expenditures for research and development are both useful instruments for the promotion of economic growth. They are not alternative instruments, however, and their relative merits or effectiveness cannot be compared. Research and development activity by its nature is directed to the future. It is in great measure abstract and, as such, often by necessity makes a minimal contribution to current economic growth.

Improvements in manufacturing methods and techniques, developed through research, serve in large part as the basis for modernization of machinery and equipment. Investment, facilitated through depreciation allowances, puts the findings of research to practical use. Consequently, one of the effects of inadequate depreciation allowances was that a great deal of the effort and resources expended in research and development was not fully utilized. Expenditures for research and for plant and equipment, therefore, are in no way opposed, rather they are complementary. Further, it should be remembered that provision is made for research spending under the tax law, just as provision is made for the replacement of facilities through depreciation.

NOTES

[1] U.S. Treasury Department, *Depreciation Guidelines and Rules*, Internal Revenue Service Publication No. 456 (7/62), p. 1.

[2] "Statement of Secretary Dillon on the New Tax Depreciation Schedules," *New York Times*, July 12, 1962, p. 14.

[3] John D. Morris, "Business Taxes are Cut 1.5 Billion by Treasury," *New York Times*, July 12, 1962, p. 15.

[4] The growth factor can be read from a Rate of Growth Conversion Table as provided in the Revenue Procedure. See Table 23.

[5] *Message From the President of the United States Relative to Our Federal Tax System*, p. 6.

[6] U.S. Department of Commerce, Office of Business Economics, July 9, 1963, USCOMM-DC-10 017.

[7] Leonard E. Morrissey, *The Many Sides of Depreciation* (Hanover, New Hampshire, 1960), pp. 4–5.

[8] Statement of Maurice E. Peloubet, "Depreciation Reform," *Tax Revision Compendium*, Compendium of Papers on Broadening the Tax Base, submitted to the House of Representatives Committee on Ways and Means, Committee Print (Washington, 1959), II, 902.

[9] Maurice E. Peloubet, "What Would Depreciation Reform Cost?," *The Tax Executive*, October 1960, pp. 38–51.

[10] *Message from the President of the United States Relative to Our Federal Tax System*, pp. 3, 6, 7.